DIVERSITY &
INCLUSION
IN EARLY
CHILDHOOD

Education at SAGE

SAGE is a leading international publisher of journals, books, and electronic media for academic, educational, and professional markets.

Our education publishing includes:

- accessible and comprehensive texts for aspiring education professionals and practitioners looking to further their careers through continuing professional development

- inspirational advice and guidance for the classroom

- authoritative state of the art reference from the leading authors in the field

Find out more at: **www.sagepub.co.uk/education**

DIVERSITY & INCLUSION IN EARLY CHILDHOOD

An Introduction

CHANDRIKA DEVARAKONDA

Los Angeles | London | New Delhi
Singapore | Washington DC

SAGE Publications Ltd
1 Oliver's Yard
55 City Road
London EC1Y 1SP

SAGE Publications Inc.
2455 Teller Road
Thousand Oaks, California 91320

SAGE Publications India Pvt Ltd
B 1/I 1 Mohan Cooperative Industrial Area
Mathura Road
New Delhi 110 044

SAGE Publications Asia-Pacific Pte Ltd
3 Church Street
#10-04 Samsung Hub
Singapore 049483

Commissioning editor: Jude Bowen
Editorial assistant: Miriam Davey
Project manager: Jeanette Graham
Assistant production editor: Thea Watson
Copyeditor: Carol Lucas
Proofreader: Isabel Kirkwood
Marketing manager: Lorna Patkai
Cover design: Wendy Scott
Typeset by: Dorwyn, Somerset, UK
Printed by: CPI Group (UK) Ltd., Croydon, CRO 4YY
Printed on paper from sustainable resources

Library of Congress Control Number:
2012937787

British Library Cataloguing in Publication data

A catalogue record for this book is available from the British Library

ISBN 978-0-85702-850-1
ISBN 978-0-85702-851-8 (pbk)

Contents

Let us pray

Dear god

We thank you in many different ways

And thank you for making us all different

If we were not varied, our lives would be plain boring

It does not matter where people come from or what religion they are

We should treat everyone equally, and not leave them out, just because they are

Different from us

Help us to appreciate every one, and how they are

Amen

By Anuradha Ponnapalli
7 years

This poem illustrates how children are inclusive and open. Although they do recognise the differences, they are happy to accept these unconditionally. They are, however, influenced by their families, peer group, practitioners and teachers from settings such as early childhood settings and schools.

This poem shows how positive experiences will enable young children to embrace diversity from a young age. This book will attempt to explore several issues around inclusion from the perspective of children, parents and practitioners.

List of figures and tables

Figures

Tables

About the author

Chandrika Devarakonda is a senior lecturer at University of Chester, UK. Her background in child development and her passion for inclusion have influenced her teaching and research interests. Her research interests lie in inclusion, children's rights, diversity and international perspectives of early childhood education. She has worked in a further education (FE) college in Manchester for 10 years teaching early childhood and health and social care courses. She has worked with disabled children in different settings, including special schools, and in community-based rehabilitation centres in India.

Acknowledgements

I would like to express my sincere gratitude to the following people who have influenced me and supported me.

I would like to thank my mother and father for being my inspiration and instilling in me good values and being my first educators. I would not have achieved much without your words of wisdom.

I would like to express my thanks to my father- and mother-in-law for being kind and supportive. My husband, Prasad, has been my pillar of strength and provided moral support. My daughter Anuradha has kept me in good cheer and enabled me to understand the concept of inclusion by sharing her experiences in the early childhood settings. All my brothers- and sisters-in-law have constantly encouraged me in this endeavour.

Professor Jeyachandran and Mrs and Mr Ramaswami have been responsible for tapping my potential, Professor Peter Farrell and Professor Peter Clough for sowing seeds of confidence and believing in me.

Thanks to my friends: Barbara Oxley for reading and commenting on my draft chapters promptly, Frances Atherton for her constant support, and Kate Wilkinson who has been inspirational and who is sadly missed. Karen Turner for all the discussions we had about inclusion and all my students on the Early Childhood Studies courses at undergraduate and postgraduate levels, who actively participated in discussions and shared their perceptions of inclusion. In addition, they constantly reminded me of the lack of a book that covered inclusion from a wider perspective that sparked the idea for this book.

I am grateful to Sage Publications, especially Jude Bowen for her enthusiasm and positive belief, sharing my vision of the book and being a constant source of encouragement, as well as Amy, Alex, Miriam, Jeanette and others for their patience and support through the whole process. I appreciate the constructive comments on the book proposal as well as draft chapters from reviewers. I would like to express my thanks to all the authors who gave permission to use their valuable work.

I would like to take this opportunity to thank everybody for making this dream come true.

Introduction

What is inclusion?

Inclusion is an elusive concept in spite of several definitions from experts, organisations and countries as well as other individuals. These definitions addressed a host of issues. Inclusion is a concept that is relevant in all countries around the world. However, the concept is interpreted in a wide range of ways. The basis for the differences is not consistent and it seems to have evolved over time.

The concept of inclusion has been defined particularly in reference to special educational needs (SEN). Ainscow (1999) argued that inclusion relates to more than children with SEN and disabilities, and is an ongoing process that does not stop at any stage. Some other definitions relate to the whole community, or to a philosophical stance linking to ethical values and beliefs.

In some countries, the terms inclusion and integration are used interchangeably. Several teachers or practitioners prefer to use integration rather than inclusion because they are more familiar with the concept (Hodkinson and Devarakonda, 2009).

The United Nations Educational, Scientific, and Cultural Organization (UNESCO) views inclusion as something that relates to those who are not able to access basic education. These children may be from disadvantaged families, Gypsy, Roma and Traveller families, ethnic minorities, families with English or other major language as an additional language, or those children who are affected by natural disasters, children with HIV/AIDS or with specific learning needs.

Allan (2008) refers to the notion that inclusion is evolving. Inclusion is a concept that has been an issue of contention between different scholars; the divergence relates to what is entailed in inclusion.

Allan (2008) commented about teachers' experiences and response to inclusion. Some were confused about how to create inclusive provision. Allan noted the frustration of a teacher being unable to account for the lack of inclusion and being answerable to children, parents, policy-makers and politicians. She warned that practitioners are guilty of being unable to include everybody appropriately as a result of failure associated with their inclusive practice, and that they are exhausted in trying to meet the diverse needs of children.

Reference is often made to highly emotive debates between the pro inclusion and pro special school experts. Both groups are influenced by their strong idealisms and are critical of each other. Inclusion is not just about schools; it is much broader and encompasses a wide range of issues from birth throughout life.

There are several definitions of inclusion that emphasise a number of issues, as the following definitions illustrate (Table I.1):

Table I.1 Analysis of definitions presented

Definition	Year	Focus of the definition	Key idea/highlight	Criticism
UNESCO	2000	Elementary education	Removing all barriers, participation, overcoming all exclusion	Focus on education
Ainscow	1999	Not only with pupils with disabilities, never-ending process	Overcoming barriers	Feasibility of practice, attitudes, wide range of people involved
Corbett and Slee	2000	Metaphor, comparison of integration and inlusion	Celebration of differences	Attitudes of practitioners to celebrate differences
Alliance for Inclusive Education	2004	Whole community	Diversity of strengths, abilities and needs	Attitudes of practitioners to focus on strengths of individuals
OFSTED	2000	Broad – to relate to different categories of children	Children from different groups	Focus on schools

- 'Inclusive education is concerned with removing all barriers to learning, and with the participation of all learners vulnerable to exclusion and marginalisation. It is a strategic approach designed to facilitate success for all children. It addresses the common goals of decreasing and overcoming all exclusion from the human right to education, at least at the elementary level, and enhancing access, participation and learning success in quality basic education for all' (UNESCO, 2000, p. 6).

- 'The agenda of inclusive education has to be concerned with over-coming barriers to participation that may be experienced by any pupils. As we have seen, however, the tendency is still to think of inclusion policy or inclusive education as being concerned only with pupils with disabilities and others categorized as having "special education needs". Furthermore, inclusion is often seen as simply involving the movement of pupils from special to mainstream contexts, with the implication that they are "included" once they are there. In contrast, I see inclusion as a never ending process rather than a simple change of state, and as dependent on continuous pedagogical and organisational development within the mainstream' (Ainscow, 1999, p. 218).

- 'An interesting metaphor presented by Corbett views integration as the square peg struggling to fit into a round hole (Corbett and Slee, 2000, p. 140). Inclusion on the other hand is treated as a circle containing many different shapes and sizes, everything relating to the whole with a caption *"Come in. We celebrate difference here. You can be yourself and not struggle to fit in"* (italics added). Inclusive education is one step ahead of integration – more assertive, life enhancing and visionary' (Corbett and Slee, 2000).

- 'A philosophy which views diversity of strengths, abilities and needs as natural and desirable, bringing to any community the opportunity to respond in ways which lead to learning and growth for the whole community and giving each and every member a valued role' (Mason, Alliance for Inclusive Education, 2004).

- According to OFSTED (2000, p. 4):

  – Its scope is broad.

  – It is about equal opportunities for all, whatever their age, gender, ethnicity, disability, attainment and background.

  – It pays particular attention to the provision made for the achievement of different groups.

Analysis of definitions presented

Inclusion and integration are two concepts that are commonly used interchangeably especially at national and international settings levels. Schneider (2009) refers to a third concept in addition to integration and inclusion. 'Common instruction' (*Gemeinsamer Unterricht*) is a term used in German settings. This concept refers to integration of special education and mainstream education. Teachers are teaching together, and children are learning with each other. In the USA, mainstreaming is a common term used to refer to inclusion, and references made to inclusion relate to education of children with disabilities. Some terms that are used which are similar to inclusion include mainstreaming, integration, normalisation, least restrictive environment, deinstitutionalisation and regular education initiative. Mainstreaming in the US refers to children with special educational needs or disabilities.

Who has a right to be included – children, parents, professionals, teachers, practitioners? Several misconceptions relate to ideas of who should be included. Several settings and practitioners around the world expect to be only for children and especially those with disabilities or SEN as the concept originally evolved.

Policy moves through different levels to reach grass-roots level where the children and their families are able to access services. The movement of policy trickling through different levels might lose the significance intended at the grass-roots level. The policy cascading from global to national, and then to regional to local and then to the early childhood setting (Figure I.1) will lead to the policy being diluted and perhaps misinterpreted. Further, the implementation of policy in the early childhood setting may not reflect the vision of the policy-maker at global or national or regional levels. As the policy-making decisions are often made at the top level and trickled down to the other levels in the hierarchy, the face of the policy may take several different shapes that may be difficult to compare with the original vision. In addition to the cultures of the individual countries having an impact on the policy at regional and local levels, an individual's attitude and the ethos of the setting might have significant impact on the implementation of the policy.

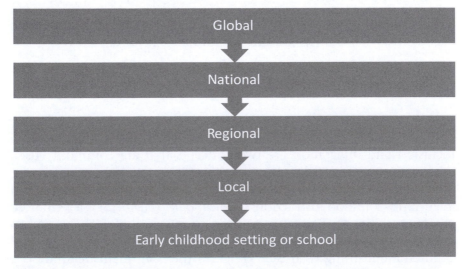

Figure I.1 The flow of the concept of inclusion policy at different levels

At global or universal level, the right to inclusive education was recommended in the Salamanca Statement and Framework for Action
(UNESCO, 1994) which expected schools to change and adapt
according to the needs of children. The UN Convention on the
Rights of Persons with Disabilities (United Nations, 2006) refers to
inclusive education as a legal right. At national level, these policies
have been embraced and have been cascaded to grass-roots or setting
level through regional and local policies.

The discussions around inclusion consistently debated how early
childhood practitioners or teachers have either referred to inclusion
as being idealistic or not realistic. In several settings, they may pay
lip-service or be tokenistic in their practice.

Arenas of inclusion/exclusion
Nutbrown and Clough (2006: 5) list a range of issues based on:

- age;
- achievement;
- challenging behaviour;
- disability;
- disaffection;
- emotional and behavioural difficulty;
- employment;
- gender;
- housing;
- language;
- mental health;
- physical impairment;
- poverty;
- race/ethnicity;
- religion;
- sexual orientation;
- social class;
- special educational need.

Inclusion as a concept has been shrouded by confusion, misunderstandings and differences of opinion, and so it remains a significant issue debated by policy-makers and practitioners at diverse levels. Inclusive education has diverse origins and influences, which include communities, activists and advocates, professional- and parent-driven movements, international governmental and non-governmental agencies.

Inclusion as a concept has been interpreted in different ways in various countries, organisations and by individuals. Inclusion means different things to different people and can often reflect stages of development of inclusive practices. Indeed, 'inclusion' can only really mean anything in practice, and there are as many versions of inclusion as there are settings, practitioners, children and families who together make up particular living and learning cultures (Clough and Nutbrown, 2006).

The definitions of inclusion encompass a range of viewpoints based on boundaries – school setting to wider society, diversity in terms of race, sex, religion, and so on, and human rights. Ainscow et al. (2006) have suggested that different definitions of inclusion can be divided into two categories – descriptive and prescriptive. Definitions of inclusion under the descriptive category relate to how inclusion is implemented in practice. Prescriptive definitions of inclusion refer to how the definition can be interpreted and used by others. Further, they have classified the ways in which the concept of inclusion has been defined in six different ways:

1. Inclusion is concerned with disabled students and others categorised as 'having special educational needs'.

2. Inclusion as a response to disciplinary inclusion.

3. Inclusion in relation to all groups seen as being vulnerable to exclusion.

4. Inclusion as developing the school for all.

5. Inclusion as 'education for all'.

6. Inclusion as a principled approach to education and society.

Corbett (2001) refers to inclusion as not only about disability but recommends schools to celebrate differences by recognising the individual needs of children (Figure I.2). Corbett (2001: 58) also refers to the 'Dump and hope model' in which placing a child in a mainstream school is not a criterion for successful inclusive education. Practitioners' references to inclusion are characterised by a sense of frustration, guilt and exhaustion, and moral panic (Allan, 2008).

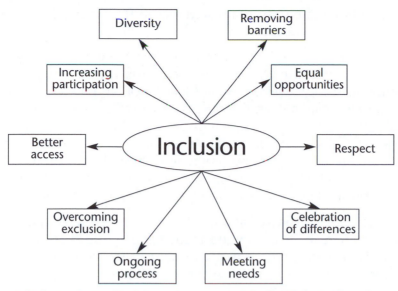

Figure I.2 Some terms that have been associated with inclusion

 Activity

In two groups, prepare for a scholarly debate by having a discussion about one of the following statements:

1. Inclusion works and is great because …
2. Inclusion is idealistic and does not work in reality.

Is this inclusion?

A setting tries to communicate with a 3-year-old bilingual child in Mandarin. The setting has a wide range of multicultural resources and displays several notices in Mandarin.

Another setting encourages other children to learn some words in Mandarin and to relate to the displays written in Mandarin. Extended family members – siblings, parents and grandparents – are invited to help decorate the setting with Chinese-style decorations.

Which practice is an example of inclusion? How can this practice be adapted to different situations in early childhood settings?

Debates and controversies

1. Is inclusion idealistic? This is how it is perceived by several practitioners and school teachers who believe it is not appropriate for

all children to be part of all activities in the setting. Is it possible to include all children fairly?

2. Inclusion is a child's right. All children have a right to go to a school that is attended by their peers and friends. This has been emphasised by several pieces of legislation and policies at global, national, regional and local level. However, children are not always able to access this right because there is a lack of access owing to location and negative attitudes towards the education of girls (especially in poor countries). In addition, some schools and early childhood settings are unable to meet the diverse and complicated needs of children with multiple disabilities.

3. Is inclusion considered as abuse? Several reports refer to inclusion of children in inappropriate mainstream settings as abuse. The needs of these children may not be met. In addition, some children may be being bullied by other children for being different.

4. Inclusion versus exclusion – the underlying principle behind providing the opportunities to access learning or meeting the needs of children would depend on the ethos of the setting as well as individual attitudes; some children may not be able to access educational opportunities because of lack of resources, funding or appropriate training for practitioners to deal with children with diverse needs.

5. Is it fair on other children that attention is focused on children with SEN and/or disabilities? Would this disadvantage those children who did not have any specific additional needs? Children with disabilities are still combating blatant educational exclusion – they account for one-third of all out-of-school children. Working children, those belonging to indigenous groups, rural populations and linguistic minorities, nomadic children and those affected by HIV/AIDS are among other vulnerable groups.

6. Is inclusive education, a concept from the North, being imposed on the rest of the world? Some indigenous communities around the world have been attributed to be inclusive. For example, a concept from Hindu philosophy is called 'vasudeiva kutumbakam' – relating to the concept of how their whole world is considered to be a big family. The term is made up of three Sanskrit words – vasudha, eva and kutumbakam. Vasudha means the earth, Eva means emphasizing and Kutumbakam means family. It means that the whole earth is just one family. The idea originates from Upanishads, an ancient Indian text, and is considered an integral part of the Hindu philosophy. Here, inclusion relates to interrelationships among people across society. The analogy of family

signifies the relationships among people highlighting together-ness. This philosophy has influenced Indian society for the past few centuries but has been muddled with several influences.

7. Is inclusive education expensive? Can poor countries afford it? Is inclusive education practical, particularly in countries with few resources?

8. Is inclusion a fashionable and politically correct concept or is it possible to implement it in all settings?

9. An effort is made to include children in mainstream settings as a result of being excluded.

10. Teacher training – how much are the teachers or practitioners prepared in their initial qualifications or training through con-tinuing professional development (CPD) or qualifications that may prepare for specific jobs around childcare? Is it feasible for a teacher or practitioner to be trained and confident to be able to meet the diverse needs of all children?

In this book

Inclusion in this book takes evidence from a wider perspective and each chapter elaborates on issues such as gender, race and culture, Gypsy, Roma and Travellers (GRT) families, English as additional lan-guage (EAL), special educational needs (SEN), and disability. Staff members working in the early childhood settings are referred to as early childhood practitioners and the settings are referred to as early childhood settings.

Several practitioners and teachers believe that inclusion is idealistic, not realistic in real-life settings. There are several teachers who believe inclusion to be a failure. Inclusion is perceived from the per-spective of children, their families (parents, carers, guardians, siblings and grandparents) and practitioners (in early childhood settings, teachers from schools).

> Civilization is the process in which one gradually increases the number of peo-ple included in the term 'we' or 'us' and at the same time decreases those labelled 'you' or 'them' until that category has no one left in it. (Howard Win-ters, 1994)

Winters relates to the concept of civilisation explicitly by referring to the notion of inclusion that appears to be simple and justified. In the current context, our society is considered to be civilised and 'every-body' included. However, there are several groups of people who find themselves to be excluded because of a variety of barriers entrenched in society. These groups include children, parents and teachers who may be engaged in including or excluding others.

Ways in which children, practitioners and parents can be included are suggested through a range of adapted appropriate resources, enabling and empowering everybody to develop to their full potential in an inclusive and mutually respected society.

Further reading

Allan, J. (2008) *Rethinking Inclusion: The Philosophers of Difference in Practice*. Dordrecht: Springer.
Nutbrown, C. and Clough, P. (2006) *Inclusion in the Early Years*. London: Sage.
Stubbs, S. (2002) *Inclusive Education: Where There Are Few Resources*. Oslo: Atlas Alliance.

Useful websites

Centre for Studies in Inclusive Education (CSIE), http://www.csie.org.uk/.
Enabling Education Network (EENET), http://www.eenet.org.uk/.
United Nations Educational, Scientific and Cultural Organization (UNESCO), http://www.unesco.org.

1

Gender and inclusion

Chapter overview

This chapter focuses on issues around inclusion in relation to gender and early childhood from the perspective of children, parents and practitioners. The stereotyping in early childhood settings is observed when children are denied access to specific resources, in how the setting is organised and the activities available. Male carers or fathers may feel ignored by the female practitioners or by mothers of other children, and male carers may be treated differently by other staff members and some parents. The rationale behind the experiences of children and adults (parents/carers and practitioners) in early childhood settings are explored in this chapter.

UNICEF (2011a: 11) has clarified that is it not enough for children to have physical access to educational settings, and explain: 'Children require not simply access to education but also equality of opportunity when in education and quality teaching to ensure enhanced learning outcomes and successful progression through education.'

Several reports highlight that girls have been excluded from education, facilities, accessing resources or curriculum. Although authentic sources claim that boys and girls have equal access to education (UNICEF, 2011b), these assertions may be shrouded by hidden discriminatory practices of practitioners as well as parents/carers. However, it is not only the practitioner but also parent(s) or carer(s) of the child, or even the child, who might prefer to be excluded from specific activities owing to their culture, religion, abilities and interests.

This chapter explores how children are excluded on the basis of their gender and what are the ways in which children can be excluded or included while conforming to orthodoxies or when challenging stereotypes. The attitudes and experiences of adults and children will influence the process of inclusion or exclusion. What are the reasons underlying the exclusion on the basis of gender? The rationale behind inclusion and exclusion on the basis of gender is influenced by several factors, such as media reports, past experiences, stereotypes, culture, expectations, peer pressure, and so on. Theories around gender identify how they influence inclusion or exclusion. An attempt is made to outline the legislation around gender that will influence practice in settings. Examples of inclusion and exclusion in early childhood settings are illustrated. Debates and controversies around gender and inclusion are identified. The challenges of defying stereotypes around gender and enabling all children to access resources and activities in the settings are discussed.

Some food for thought

Does the gender of a child influence what it means to be a child, how a child plays, how society constructs childhood especially expectations from girls and boys? From the perspective of an early years practitioner, does it matter if the practitioner is a male or a female, do employers provide opportunities for women and men to become childcare practitioners, are men restricted in their roles and responsibilities towards children and their families? Do the stereotypical attitudes and beliefs of a practitioner influence their practice in relation to children and their family members?

There are also issues around a parent's perspective – are fathers and mothers treated the same by the practitioner? Do practitioners (who are traditionally female) prefer to communicate with men or women as carers of children and are they explicit about their attitudes on a day-to-day basis? What about single parents and same-sex couples?

What are the stereotypical ways in which gender is the basis for exclusion? Are children pushed towards conforming to the society's stereotypes? What is the major influence – is it nature or nurture that drives a child to be compliant to the expectations of the society? Is it possible to mould a child to challenge the stereotypes dictated by the society? What is the impact of media and technology, peer group, local cultures and expectations of the society on inclusion and exclusion on children?

Contexts of inclusion and exclusion

It is important to clarify the differences between gender and sex as these terms are used interchangeably. These concepts have been defined from social and biological perspectives.

Sex and gender

The term 'sex' usually refers to the biological and physiological characteristics that are used to define men and women. 'Gender' on the other hand, is a socially constructed concept relating to roles, acceptable behaviour, and activities and attributes that a given society considers appropriate for men and women. Male and female are sex categories, while masculine and feminine are gender categories. Owing to the differences in culture, aspects of gender may vary greatly in different societies, while aspects of sex will not vary generally between different societies. It is more common to use gender differences as a blanket term for sex and gender differences.

It has been realised that gender and sex are often used in literature by authors and practitioners interchangeably with similar meaning. However, it will be useful to clarify the meaning of these two concepts and how these two concepts are defined from sociological as well as biological perspectives.

A definition from the World Health Organization (WHO) clearly distinguishes between gender and sex. '"Gender" is used to describe those characteristics of women and men, which are socially constructed, while sex refers to those which are biologically determined. People are born female or male but learn to be girls and boys who grow into women and men. This learned behaviour makes up gender identity and determines gender roles' (World Health Organization, 2002: 4).

 Points for reflection

- What are the ways in which a child, a practitioner or a parent can be included or excluded in an early childhood setting? Reflect on your childhood experiences and discuss the ways in which boys and girls were included or excluded in a setting.

Continues

Continued

- Consider the factors that influenced or caused a barrier.
- How does your reflection on your childhood experiences of inclusion and exclusion compare with the experience of children in the contemporary context? What are the significant differences?
- Presentation of activities and layout of environment can restrict access by children (boys/girls) due to stereotyping.
- Girls or boys are usually engaged in gender stereotypical play.
- Attitudes of employers and parents can prevent a male practitioner from being recruited or taking a specific caring role.
- Practitioners may stereotype parents' role in care of their children – mothers are given more opportunities to access information about their child; fathers are overlooked by female practitioners.
- Parents prefer a female practitioner to a male practitioner to take care of their child/ren.

Parents may tend to encourage stereotypical play and not be happy about challenging stereotypes. Some parents insist on their children (especially boys) being involved in traditional stereotypical activities in an early years setting. Girls are encouraged to play with dolls and 'home-making' types of play. They are also encouraged to be less active than boys, for example, sitting colouring/looking at books – and not getting their clothes messy! Girls who play against their stereotype are labelled 'tomboys'. Girls engaged in non-stereotypical activities are widely accepted whereas several parents express reservations when boys do the same.

 Activity

What are the expectations for girls and boys in different societies/countries? Relate this to behaviour, dress code, play and education. How does it change in different generations and in different cultures as well as geographical locations?

Chat with people from different generations, cultures and countries about their childhood and analyse the impact of external factors and differences in the expectations for boys and girls.

Discuss any stereotypes that promoted exclusion. Were girls and boys excluded from specific situations? How did it influence the child's holistic development?

It is common practice to have gender-based stereotypical expectations of children, for practitioners as men or women and as parents. Children pick stereotypes from their environment – parents, early childhood settings, their peer group and early childhood practitioners – as role models. Practitioners and teachers may not be aware that they are excluding a child or stereotyping, as it has been a 'normal' practice. For example, a nursery teacher in a foundation stage would not have realised a 4-year-old child's dilemma when she related the following to her parents at the end of the day: 'When I was in nursery, our teacher asked us to copy a letter to Santa requesting a Christmas present. All children had to copy what the practitioner wrote on the board: girls – Barbie, and boys – a car!' The child, a girl, further added that she really did not want a Barbie from Santa! Is this teacher promoting stereotyping and encouraging children to conform? A child's own choice is not allowed, resulting in low self-respect and confidence. However, some settings are encouraging practitioners to be open and flexible, to change their practice by giving opportunities for children to express themselves positively.

Children and gender

Shepherd (2010) reports that girls as young as 4 believed that they are 'cleverer, more successful and hardworking' than boys. This belief is accepted by boys at a later age. The study further pointed to this supporting the principle of self-fulfilling prophecy that may be the reason for boys' perceptions.

Freeman (2007) reports another study that demonstrated that children aged 3 years were able to distinguish between girls and boys. Five-year-old children were rigidly following gender stereotypes more than their 3-year-old counterparts. This may be a result of the response of their parents to their cross-gender play. Adults' approval or disapproval of their children's choice of toys or games may influence children's stereotypical or non-stereotypical attitudes.

Are gifts for children stereotypical – driven by gender of the child? When a newborn baby is given gifts, do they have to be in gender-specific colours – pink for girls and blue for boys – is this hype created by society, media or markets?

Market research provides evidence of promoting gendered play. For example Mattel's website (https://shop.mattel.com/checkout/index.jsp?process=login) has toys categorised under gender. Some of the examples include:

Boy – Action figures and accessories, Electronics games and puzzles, Lifestyle party supplies, Role-play vehicles.

Girl – Dolls and accessories, Dress-up DVDs, Electronics games and Puzzles, Party supplies, Role-play apparel subscriptions.

Does this encourage children and their parents to stick to the limits suggested by Mattel? Further, when a toy shop is visited, sometimes it can be seen that toys for girls and boys are in separate locations and boldly coloured in pink and blue, forcing parents to comply with the traditional stereotypes. Is this pushing children to conform?

Practitioners and gender

Traditionally, childcare practitioners are predominantly females. Early childhood education remains one of the most gender-skewed of all occupations. This has been a global phenomenon with statistics pointing to 2–6 per cent male practitioners mainly involved as play workers or in after-school clubs or as childcare practitioners in outdoor settings (Children's Workforce Development Council (CWDC), 2009). At least 9 per cent of settings employ at least one male childcare practitioner. Lack of male childcare practitioners has been reported not only in the UK but all over the world. In developing and underdeveloped countries a male childcare practitioner is not even considered an option. As working in childcare has not traditionally been considered as a job for men, several governments are challenging the stereotype by inviting men to work in childcare settings. The reasons for poor recruitment of men as childcare practitioners are that it is non-traditional, has low pay and poor status, there are fears for the safety of children and the stigma of possibly being a paedophile.

Women are overrepresented in the early childhood workforce as well as in primary schools. For example, in the Netherlands 85 per cent of the teachers are women; in the UK it is 86 per cent and in Denmark 76 per cent (Peeters, 2007). In 2002 the government of the Flemish community of Belgium approved new regulations recommending childcare settings to hire males as well as females, as well as ethnic minorities, as childcare workers, and increased the salaries in the day-care centres by 30 per cent. The government has replaced the name with a more gender-neutral name for the care profession. The reference to care in the name of the worker was replaced by a more pedagogic word, 'kinderverzorger' or 'child carer' became 'kinderbegeleider' or 'companion of children'.

In order to support new male childcare practitioners, a number of local authorities in the UK offer a male mentor to new male childcare workers/teachers and student trainees. In Norway the male childcare workers have their own association that organises meetings and social activities where trainees and experienced childcare workers can meet and talk about their work (Hauglund, 2005, cited by Peeters, 2007). In Belgium and New Zealand, all male childcare practitioners were invited to a meeting and a national network for male teachers is being set up.

Another interesting example from Belgium (cited by Peeters, 2007) illustrated how early childhood training could be made more attractive to men by modifying the pedagogue course in the Kolding Paedagogseminarium (Wohlgemuth, 2003, cited by Peeters, 2007). They introduced the option of 'sport and outdoor activities' in their pedagogue course, at undergraduate level. The number of male students opting for 'sports and outdoor activities' was 50 per cent and the total number of male students in the institute rose from less than 15 per cent to 24 per cent.

Several experts have recommended 'multiplicity of gendered identities' (Cameron et al., 1999) in relation to gender, ethnicity and culture. It has been reported that the employment of diverse practitioners is a norm in some settings such as the Sheffield Children's Centre, and the Pen Green centre prides itself on its gender-neutral policy. It has been recognised that male practitioners are not only role models for children but also for their fathers, in addition to making the centre father-friendly.

Tavvecchio (2003, cited by Peeters, 2007) reported that the response of male and female teachers to the rough and tumble behaviour of boys varied significantly. While male practitioners related the boisterous behaviour to 'boyish' nature, female practitioners related the same to being aggressive. The proportion of the number of women working with children is higher in settings where younger children are cared for (Moss, 2003).

The British government tried to target men by raising awareness of men working in childcare in their national childcare recruitment campaign in 2000. In 2011, only 2 per cent of males were working with children under 5 in contrast to the target of 6 per cent. Norway was much more positive, expecting to recruit 20 per cent of males to work with young children. However, Norway's government's strong commitment and policy helped to recruit only 9 per cent of men (Johanssen, 2007, cited by Peeters, 2007). An increasing proportion of men are enrolled in professional childcare courses. In Denmark, men form 25 per cent of enrolled students on professional courses. In 2009, 7 per cent of childcare practitioners were males working in centres for under 3s, 11 per cent in kindergartens for 3–6 year-olds, and 13 per cent in mixed age centres for children from birth to 6 years. This has been as a result of the increasing number of males gaining qualifications and training as professionals. Further, a broader professional perspective provided more options and pathways for promotion in addition to positive employment conditions with job security and a better salary. In Germany, men accounted for 3.4 per cent of early childhood practitioners. The numbers in urban areas are higher, at 9 per cent (Oberhuemer, 2011).

The absence of men in the early childhood sector would reinforce the notion that it is mainly women who are responsible for the emotional, social and intellectual development of young children. On the other hand, male practitioners have often presented the curriculum and environment from a different perspective that has attracted children's attention.

Male practitioners provided positive role models to those children from single-mother families. Ninety-eight per cent of mothers and fathers were in favour of men caring for children between the ages of 3 and 5 in 2009 compared with 55 per cent in 2005. Currently, less than 3 per cent of nursery staff are men (CWDC, 2009).

Men may sometimes present a threat to female practitioners because they may progress earlier in their careers just by being male. They may also be perceived by some parents to be a potential threat to young children.

Although men are underrepresented in the early years sector, it has been reported that a male practitioner may struggle to be accepted by parents as an efficient practitioner as a result of challenging the stereotype. Male practitioners often express frustration at being excluded by the management and other practitioners when they are not allowed to help in some childcare contexts, for example, to change nappies or to be solely responsible for taking care of children after the regular working hours.

The Children's Workforce Development Council (CWDC, 2009) reported the results of a survey that urged men to take childcare jobs so that young children will have male role models. The survey also indicated that single mothers would like their children to have male role models. It has been revealed that 36 per cent of children had fewer than six hours per week of contact with a male and 17 per cent have fewer than two hours a week.

The CWDC (2009) research reported children may be conforming to societal pressures that they pick up from their family, which is showcased in their behaviour during play or their responses to stories or other contexts of the day. It also reported that children from single-parent families, especially single mother families, lack positive male role models. Fifty-five per cent of parents wished that a male practitioner cared for their child. This research further reported that it is not only male role models that the mothers are looking for. In addition, men are believed to offer a different set of skills for, for example, playing outdoors, allowing children to be independent, and being more friendly with children (Brandth and Kvande, 1998) Further, 37 per cent of parents believe male practitioners will set boys a good example, while a quarter say they believe boys will behave better with a man (CWDC, 2009).

Parents and gender

Trends such as divorce and remarriage, as well as more women having children outside marriage, result in a weakening of the role of fathers in the lives of their children. Practitioners from early childhood settings who are predominantly women are likely to communicate with mothers rather than fathers due to their stereotypical perception of mothers as the primary carers of children. With an increase in the numbers of children in single-parent families (usually living with mothers) and the predominance of female childcare practitioners, many children lack positive male role models.

Fathers who are carers and especially those who head single-parent families may find themselves excluded. The Fatherhood Institute website has several case studies of good practice that have involved fathers in diverse ways. Peters et al. (2008) found British mothers only a little more likely than fathers (53 per cent versus 45 per cent) to say they feel 'very involved' in their child's education. A UK survey (Peters et al., 2008) found 70 per cent of two-parent family fathers and 81 per cent of non-resident parents (mainly men) wanted to be more involved in their children's education.

In contrast to father's involvement in developed countries, fathers among the Aka Pygmies, who live in a tropical forest in the African Congo, are considered to be most involved with their infants, spending at least 47 per cent of their time with their infants. They pick up, cuddle and play with their babies at least five times more than fathers in other societies.

Kahn (2006) has conducted several research studies into how fathers can be successfully engaged in childcare settings, and developed four models to engage fathers:

1. Inclusive communication – practitioners are encouraged to use language that enables fathers to feel included in the setting. They have to use a range of language skills such as verbal, non-verbal and written language to attract fathers to become involved in the early childhood setting.

2. Father-directed activities – organise activities when it is convenient for the fathers to attend, for example over a weekend. Use technology such as sending reminders through text or email to remind them about forthcoming events.

3. Gender talk included challenging gender stereotyping and encouraging fathers to participate in the settings. This model suggests that if practitioners consider fathers to be primarily the breadwinners and secondarily to be carers of their children, the fathers may not realise the importance of their involvement in the early childhood settings.

4. 'Fathers matter' leaflet – this leaflet included issues and activities that would be appropriate to engage fathers in settings.

It has been found that fathers and mothers are both important and influence children's development. Research suggests that children do better educationally, psychologically and socially when fathers are actively involved. 'Fathers matter' is a guidance leaflet produced by Kahn that provided some ideas and tips on how to involve fathers in an early childhood setting. Some settings plan specific activities for fathers as they are considered to be hard to reach owing to their long working hours, and maternal gatekeeping.

Gender and culture

Exclusion of girls: although parents are protective of their pre-school-aged sons and daughters, in some communities there is more concern about girls' in-class safety as well as their safety walking to and from pre-school, especially in some developing as well as under-developed countries and particularly if they have to travel long distances to get to school. Unless older siblings or other escorts are available, girls may be excluded. In families where sons are valued more than daughters and the family is unable or unwilling to fund the education of all their children, daughters may be deprived of early childcare and education (ECCE) or be given the lower-cost, and often the lower-quality, option. If a girl is characterised by multiple categories of disadvantage such as being poor, disabled, belonging to an ethnic minority group, and living in a rural area, then this child is more likely to be excluded than a boy. Further, some cultural groups may prefer to exclude their child from attending a school because of safety concerns of their girls in school (lack of gender-specific and clean toilets in a setting) as well as when walking to and from school (Sharma, 2010).

The stereotypes are promoted in some cultures in which girls are not encouraged to go to school as the assumption is that they could develop caring skills at home rather than at school. So parents of these girls would prevent them from attending a school. On the other hand, families may not have access to a school close by. If the school is far away, parents may decide against sending their daughters to a distant school for fear of safety of the girls. This supports the theory that girls are weak and boys are strong. Girls are discouraged from attending schools in Asian and African cultures owing to girls having less access to schools in rural and poor areas. This might result in the girls and boys conforming to the societal expectations and roles when they become adults for the reasons stated above.

Theoretical base

There are several theoretical perspectives of gender. One of these perspectives is viewed 'as fluid, socially constructed and continually negotiated, rather than a biologically determined binary divide' (Sumison, 2005: 115).

Brain and gender

Is there any difference in the brains of males and females? Are there differences between the maturation of girls and boys? What is influencing children's behaviour – nature or nurture? These questions have been strongly contested/debated by researchers and educationists. It has been argued that there are differences in the brains of girls and boys: male brains are bigger than female brains, resulting in boys being intellectually superior. This discourse drew a lot of scepticism and is inconclusive, and is not supported by evidence which shows that girls do better than boys in education at different levels.

Women can be dominant left-hemisphere of the brain resulting in better linguistic skills and males can be right-hemisphere dominant resulting in better visuo-spatial skills. Does this explain boys' obsession with cars and blocks and girls being attracted to the home corner to play with kitchens or dolls? This is further complemented by research that indicates that a lot of girls are able to speak clearly at 3 years, whereas boys do not speak clearly until they are 4½.

Further, how do society and media influence practitioners and parents to embrace stereotypes – boys as noisy, strong, physical, energetic, rough and boisterous, and girls as caring, soft, organised and weak – and promote the same by their provision of environment and resources to children at home and in an early childhood setting?

Functionalism theorists believed that the division of responsibilities between males and females has been entrenched owing to its bene-fit to society. Conflict theory states: 'If men can prevent women from developing their potential then they can maintain the status quo. If men keep the traditional division of labour, men continue to enjoy the privileges they have.' Conflict theorists see the traditional roles as outdated and inappropriate for an industrial society. Women who prefer to enter career fields that were reserved for men have the right to make that choice, regardless of whether it is functional to society. Symbolic interactionists focus on how boys and girls learn 'how they are supposed to act'. This process is called gender socialisation; gen-der is acquired in a large part from interaction with parents, teachers and peers, as well as through the mass media.

There are some theories that propose how children develop their gender identity. These theories are influenced by some popular theorists such as Piaget and Vygotsky.

Social learning theory: children learn their behaviour from their envi-ronment. Children are influenced by adults' (parents' and practitioners') use of language and behaviour. This can result from reinforcement provided by adults in response to children's behaviour.

Kohlberg's (1966) development of gender identity: a child develops an understanding of gender in various stages. As the child grows older, their understanding of gender is more complex. Gender iden-tity is the first stage, in which a child is able to correctly identify themselves based on their own sex, and is usually reached by the age of 2 years. The second stage is gender stability in which a child realises that their gender remains the same across time, and is usu-ally reached by the age of 4 years. At this stage, external features such as hair and clothing influence their understanding. The third stage refers to gender constancy, which is usually reached by 7 years. In this stage the child starts to understand that gender is constant irrespective of external features.

Munroe et al. (1984) conducted a cross-cultural study and found that children in several cultures had the same sequence of stages in gender development.

Bem (1993) links both cognitive and socialisation theories. Children form categories of gender influenced by the existing categories in contemporary society. She argues that parents around children transmit on a social constructionist approach perceives gender acquisition as a result of external influences. Bem has identified three key 'gender lenses': gender polarisation (men and women are different), androcentrism (males are superior to females) and biological essentialism (the first two lenses are a result of biological differences between the sexes).

Children may develop stereotypical attitudes as a result of being put into orthodox learning environments and as adults they may not challenge the traditional perceptions of being a man or a woman guided by the societal norms.

Gender schema theory: children learn about being male and female from the culture in which they live. This theory suggests that children adjust their behaviour to fit in with the gender norms and expectations of their culture.

There are some feminists who strongly reject gender stereotypes and bring up their children defying the traditional stereotypes. Risman and Myers (1997) conducted their research on children living in feminist and egalitarian households, specifically focusing on their gender performances, ideologies and attitudes. The authors suggested that parenting styles and philosophies have an influence on children, although they may be conflicting with stereotypes provided in schools, churches, the media and by their peers.

Legislation

Legislation around the world exists to promote equality in relation to gender. The legislation around gender mainly highlights the way males and females are treated differently, resulting in exclusion from certain key aspects of the setting in the context of exclusion and inclusion. In response to a significant number of girls not accessing education, the United Nations Girls Education Initiative (UNGEI) was launched in 2000 to ensure all children are able to complete primary schooling.

Until 1 October 2010, gender equality was emphasised by law in different legislation. One of the earliest pieces of legislation in the UK that recommended equality of sexes was the Equal Pay Act 1970. This law prohibits any less favourable treatment between men and women in terms of pay and conditions of employment across any sector. However, statistics recognise that even in the current context there are differences in pay between the sexes with similar qualifications and experience (Pike, 2011).

The Sex Discrimination Act 1975 protects men and women from discrimination on the grounds of sex or marriage. The Act concerned employment, training, education, harassment, the provision of goods and services, and the disposal of premises. This Act was replaced by the Equality Act 2010 on 1 October 2010.

The Equality Act provides a modern, single legal framework with clear, streamlined law to tackle disadvantage and discrimination effectively. This Act extends to and includes gender reassignment and sexual orientation, as well as sex, which are some of the protected characteristics.

The Equality Act 2010 is law in England, Scotland and Wales, and brings together all existing legislation around discrimination. This legislation defines some of the protected characteristics, and recommends that all categories of people listed under protected characteristics are shielded from discrimination. This legislation hopes to bring in positive changes in the practice in early childhood settings, and will have significant impact on the employers and service providers. The changes could relate to recruitment policies, as well as ensuring equality of access for children and families, positive role models, reviewing attitudes of practitioners, and effective communication with parents and carers as well as professionals.

Examples of good practice

The policy and practice of settings should reflect anti-discrimination, challenge stereotypes and positively value diversity. All early childhood settings must ensure children have equal access to a curriculum, both indoors and outdoors, which supports and extends learning and develops their understanding, skills and knowledge.

All carers – mothers, fathers, grandparents or others – must be valued and respected. A partnership between parents (or other carers) and practitioners will need to be embedded in all practice to ensure equal value is placed on involving them irrespective of their gender.

Continuing training and professional development should be available and accessible to enable all early years practitioners to build on previous training and qualifications to sustain the quality of their practice through review and reflection. Settings should develop policies that actively facilitate the involvement of all staff in appropriate training, development and education opportunities. There should be an attempt to attract recruitment and retention of underrepresented groups, especially men.

 Case study

A conversation between two 5-year-old children (a girl and a boy) in the school:

Lisa: Did you see the fire engine today in the school?

Matte: Yes, I did.

Lisa: Wasn't it exciting? I would love to go on it. It was very fascinating to see the firemen showing us how to splash water on the objects on fire … I would like to be a fireman – no firewoman when I grow up!!!!

Matte: No, you cannot as girls can't be fireman. Don't you see it is FIREMAN AND NOT FIREWOMAN!!! Have you ever seen a firewoman or heard about a firewoman in a story? You are silly!!!

Lisa: But I will be a fireperson when I grow up! What if we do not know any woman being a fireman! It is silly – it should be a FIREPERSON and not a FIREMAN. Do you remember, in the programme 'Bob the Builder' we saw Bob building with Wendy's help …?

The conversation was stopped when they saw their teacher behind them.

As their teacher, how will you encourage the boy to understand that girls can be firepersons too?

How can the teacher promote gender equity in the setting?

How can this be embedded into the curriculum of the class which these two children belong to?

What should be the plan of action of the teacher to follow up?

Best practice ideas

As an early childhood practitioner:

- Do you meet the individual needs of all children?

- Do you ensure you provide positive images of gender to children in their daily routines?

- Do you ensure all children have access to all resources in the setting challenging gender stereotypes?

- Do you ensure the setting communicates and provides opportunities for both parents of the child to be involved?

- Does the setting make sure they provide appropriate opportunities for practitioners (males and females) in the recruitment process as well as meeting the needs of children?

- Do you challenge any prejudice or discrimination by children or adults?

- Are children provided with non-stereotypical activities in the early childhood settings?

- Do you have informal chats with children and their families on gender and stereotyping?

- Do you encourage young children to reflect upon what it means for them to be 'a boy' or 'a girl'?

- Do you encourage them to broaden their interests/activities – adaptation of the layout and use of the setting itself to challenge existing gender stereotypes and patterns of behaviour (posters and displays, use of and access to resources and materials), books to portray males and females in a positive way?

- Does your setting organise a 'dad's stay and play' session on a Saturday when dads can bring their children and join their children in nursery activities?

- Is there a role-play area to attract boys and girls with appropriate resources and materials?

- Do you challenge traditional stereotypes – invite parents engaged in non-traditional roles such as male nurses, female police officers, firewomen, show films that depict characters of men and women in challenging traditional and stereotypical roles?

Debates and controversies

Nature versus nurture – gendered play – is it nature or nurture that influences boys and girls to play games that they are naturally inclined to or are they driven by stereotypes, for example boys in rough and tumble play and girls in caring roles in role play situations or with dolls? How much does an early childhood setting influence a child to develop stereotypical roles?

Practitioners – males versus females – traditionally, females are early childhood practitioners. But, who makes a better practitioner? What are the reasons for men not being employed as childcarers? Are they not accepted or do they not feel inspired to be a childcarer? Research and literature report that male practitioners are not allowed to take care of children in their groups (Owen, 2003), for example, changing nappies, or some settings ensure a female carer is included in the rota of caring for children when a male practitioner is responsible. A female carer is allowed to take sole care of children while some males are not. Some parents are apprehensive when their baby or child is taken care of by a male carer. Do the low status of being a childcare practitioner and the poor pay and conditions not attract males as early childhood practitioners? Are males apprehensive of being accused of being a paedophile by parents? Is there discrimination in male and female early childhood practitioners in relation to their pay? Do males get better pay compared to their female colleagues?

Stereotypes – are children encouraged or given opportunities to access resources, activities, play or curriculum subjects or environment? Does the early childhood setting expose children to non-stereotypical resources or positive role models of both genders?

 Points for reflection

Reflect on your own experiences as a child or practitioner or student in placement or as a parent of a child attending an early childhood setting. Consider if the setting is inclusive.

Implications for practice

All children need to have opportunities where they can develop a range of skills reflecting their potential. Children will relate to non-sexist roles and responsibilities. Accept and respect differences, morals and values. Children are stereotyped as a result of society's attitudes and an expectation of what is supposed to be a girl or a boy. If these expectations conflict with the traditional stereotypes as a result of moving to another country, parents may be hesitant and not confident enough to challenge stereotypes.

Parents should be given opportunities to articulate their opinions about the quality of their child's experiences. Parents should be motivated to engage in pre-school activities and to collaborate with childcare practitioners irrespective of their gender.

Provide diverse opportunities for parents to challenge stereotypes. Give both parents opportunities to participate in the activities of the setting. Be aware of the values and beliefs of parents and raise their awareness of their role in continuing care. Ensure children receive messages at home that are reflecting, and not conflicting with, those received in the childcare settings. Ensure communication sent to parents uses non-sexist language.

Practitioners have to get opportunities to share good practice with other practitioners in their authorities. Do the settings offer opportunities for their staff members to update their knowledge and understanding of gender and inclusion? Provide opportunities for men and women to be recruited in the early childhood settings.

 Research issues

Some areas of published research that have been conducted around gender include:

- Does a childcare practitioner's gender influence their role and effectiveness in Children's Services?
- Are children's choices of activities influenced by gender stereotypes?
- Does gender influence achievement?
- What are the risks taken by girls and boys in play?
- Involvement of fathers in pre-school settings.
- Is gendered play a result of nature or nurture?
- Do learning styles of girls and boys influence their success and achievement?
- Do boys miss male role models in early childhood settings?
- The influence of media on gendered play.

This section refers to research published around some significant issues around gender. The abstract for each research document is followed by some questions that will stimulate thinking and critical analysis of findings.

Refer to this link for some interesting case studies: 'Engaging boys in the Early Years: the experiences of three Islington settings' at

http://www.islington.gov.uk/DownloadableDocuments/
EducationandLearning/Pdf/PSEYT_engaging_boys_early_years.pdf.

Practitioners and students on placement could collaborate to evaluate these innovative ways to engage children in non-stereotypical activities to promote their holistic development.

Holland (2000) 'Take the toys from the boys? An examination of the genesis of policy and the appropriateness of adult perspectives in the area of war, weapon and superhero play', *Citizenship, Social and Economic Education*, 4(2): 92–108.

This article considers the genesis of a zero tolerance approach to war, weapon and superhero play in early years settings in the UK over the past 30 years. This exploration is located in the development of anti-sexist perspectives and concerns about effective early intervention in the spiral of male violence and it is suggested that this has resulted in the 'Othering' of young boys in settings where this policy is enforced. Research challenging assumptions about the connection between war, weapon and superhero play and aggressive behaviour is discussed, and the possible benefits of a more relaxed approach to these areas of play, which are more consistent with Scandinavian notions of gender pedagogy, are highlighted.

- List the key issues from the article. Does the author present her arguments around zero tolerance in a balanced way?
- Find any follow-up research that has been inspired from this article.
- Have there been any significant changes in the attitudes of practitioners towards zero tolerance in the past 10 years?
- What is the relevance of this article in other countries?
- What are the limitations of this article?

Sumsion, J. (2005) 'Male teachers in early childhood education: issues and case study', *Early Childhood Research Quarterly*, 20: 109–23.

Much of the debate about the desirability or otherwise, of attempting to address the gender imbalance in the early childhood teaching profession has been limited by a reliance on rhetoric rather than empirical evidence. The purpose of this article is to assist in shifting this debate to a more empirical basis by reporting findings from an exploratory empirical investigation of children's perceptions and gender positioning of their male pre-school teacher. Children's drawings of their teacher and accompanying text generated in conversational interviews were analysed inductively with the intent of gaining preliminary insights into whether the presence of a male teacher might challenge their gender stereotypes. Children focused mostly on typical teacher roles. Traditional gender roles and attributes were reflected in their play. While it is difficult to draw

Continues

Continued

definite conclusions from the study, for these children the presence of a male teacher did not appear to disrupt gender stereotypes.

- List the key findings of this research.
- What is the relevance of this research in other countries?
- Can this study be replicated in your setting with similar results and conclusions?
- What are the strengths of the methods used to obtain data and analyse findings?
- What are the limitations of this research?

Further reading

Browne, N. (2004) *Gender Equity in the Early Years*. Maidenhead: Open University Press.

Holland, P. (2003) *We Don't Play with Guns Here: War, Weapon and Superhero Play in the Early Years*. Maidenhead: Open University Press.

MacNaughton, G. (2000) *Rethinking Gender in Early Childhood Education*. London: Sage.

Risman, B.J. and Myers, K. (1997) 'As the twig is bent: children reared in feminist households', *Qualitative Sociology*, 20(2): 229–52.

Roberts-Holmes, G.P. (2011) 'Working with men as colleagues in the early years: issues and ways forward', in L. Miller and C. Cable (eds) *Professionalism, Leadership and Management in the Early Years*. London: Sage.

Thorne, B. (1993) *Gender Play: Girls and Boys in School*. New Brunswick, NJ: Rutgers University Press.

Useful websites

Equality Human Rights, http://www.equalityhumanrights.com/.

Preschool Learning Alliance, http://www.pre-school.org.uk/practitioners/inclusion.

Fatherhood Institute, http://www.fatherhoodinstitute.org/.

Men in Childcare, www.meninchildcare.co.uk.

2

Race and inclusion

Chapter overview

This chapter discusses the role of race in inclusion and exclusion and how race is addressed in early childhood contexts from the perspectives of children, their parents or carers and practitioners.

Race has always been considered to be a complicated concept. Some children from ethnic minority groups may be confused about their identity – as one 4-year-old Indian girl asked her mum: 'Am I going to be an English lady or an Indian lady when I grow up?' Further, when students on a BA Early Childhood Studies course were asked the question: 'How would you like to describe yourself?' it was considered to be a thought-provoking question to answer by almost everybody, irrespective of their background being white, black, mixed heritage, or other. Some students preferred to refer themselves as English, Scottish or Welsh or British or European. On the other hand, people who migrated from other countries, and in spite of having acquired British citizenship, were still comfortable to refer to themselves as belonging to their original country of birth.

This chapter explores the concept of race and inclusion in early childhood settings – from the perspectives of children, practitioners and parents. The concepts of ethnicity and race have always been used interchangeably and sometimes confused, with some links made to religion, especially in the case of Jews and Muslims. Some of the terms related to race and ethnic minorities are explored in relation to their appropriate meanings, the problems around the usage of these terms and the terms preferred. Several issues around race have been contested, such as the concept of race, self-identity, and little or lack of awareness of other ethnic groups. Are some terms – ethnic minority, minority ethnic or black – used to refer to people who are labelled black or is the word 'black' used to denote everybody other than those who are 'white'? People do not prefer to be labelled as black in spite of being non-white. Skin colour may be differently described as white, black, brown and yellow.

A conversation on race:

> In a multi-cultural setting, a group of 4-year-old children consisting of a Korean, Pakistani, Nigerian and English were engrossed in a conversation about race. They were overheard illustrating and analysing the concept of race by relating to differences and similarities. They concluded that there were four different types of people in the world whose skin colour was black, brown, yellow and white. They commented that although skin colour, hair and facial features are different, there are similarities too in terms of colour of blood (red) and teeth (white).

Statistics

The UK is becoming ethnically diverse, it has been predicted that in the 2011 Census, the population of ethnic minorities in the UK will increase from 7.9 per cent to 15 per cent. As a result of failing political and economic situations in certain countries in the past, in Somalia, Kenya, Uganda and, recently, Afghanistan, Iraq, Egypt and Libya the native population have been forced to seek refuge in other countries for their own safety. As a result of moving to a new country with different cultures and constructions of childhood, children and their families have to familiarise themselves with the expectations and may also have to deal with being stereotyped or discriminated against.

The BBC (2009a) reported the Office for National Statistics projecting the UK population to rise from 61 million to 71.6 million by 2033. If current trends in growth continue, just over two-thirds of this increase in population is a result of migration directly or indirectly.

It has been estimated that the ethnic minority population will double in the next 50 years. In one BBC (2010) report it has been predicted that 'Groups outside the white British majority are increasing in size and share, not just in the areas of initial migration, but throughout the country, and our projections suggest that this trend is set to continue through to 2051'. In this situation it is highly likely that there will be many children from ethnic minority families accessing the early childhood settings and so it will be extremely important to ensure that all children and their families feel included.

Census 2011

Wallop (2011) reported a 2.5 million increase in population as a result of migration and a higher birth rate in families from ethnic minorities. Rogers (2011) reported in the *Guardian*, that the non-white British population has grown from 6.6 million in 2001 to 9.1 million in 2009. The non-white British population has grown by 4.1 per cent owing to the influx of Eastern Europeans as well as people migrating from Australia and New Zealand to the UK. The report also highlights an increase in the number of people identifying themselves as mixed population by almost 50 per cent and this is not due to an increase in birth rates but is as a result of 'the population is mixing more'. The 2011 Census (ONS, 2011a) added new categories such as Welsh, English and Cornish in addition to the Gypsy or Irish Traveller families and Arabs added as 'any other ethnic group'.

Definition and terminology

Black refers to children of Black Caribbean; Black African; mixed White and Black Caribbean and mixed White and Black African heritage. Practitioners should find out about individual children's backgrounds from their families because the various terms used to identify black children incorporate a range of different heritages, histories, and experiences.

Asians – this term has been interpreted in various ways in different countries. In the UK, the term 'Asian' is referred to people belonging to South Asian origin – Indians, Pakistanis, Bangladeshis and Sri Lankans. In the UK census forms, 'Asian' and 'Chinese' are recorded as separate. This term has connotations in different countries.

The census form in 2011 introduced some new categories such as Welsh, English and Cornish.

Contexts of inclusion and exclusion

Race is characterised by physical characteristics, such as colour of skin and colour and shape of eyes and hair. How and why do children get excluded by children and adults on the basis of their skin colour, nationality or religion? Is this blatantly visible or covert? Is this evident through their attitudes, behaviour, language used or using appropriate resources, providing access to environment? Are people with fair skin at an advantage because society assigns them power and control? Do children with fair skin from other European countries living in England face any issues around exclusion?

Race and ethnicity are always considered sensitive issues as everybody prefers to be thought of as politically correct so that they do not offend anybody by using offensive language. Jane Lane warns that when referring to terminology around race there is no right or wrong terminology, but intentions not to offend the individual. 'It is sometimes difficult to know what terms/words to use when we are talking about issues around racial equality and to be confident about using them. Some people may feel anxious or unsure about using the "correct" or "right" word or term and, consequently, may try to avoid using them at all' (Lane, 2006b).

What are the ways in which children get excluded? Are adults more inclined to exclude because of their rigid notions of stereotypes? For example, an experienced practitioner from a predominantly white community may express reservations about their ability to meet the needs (especially, language, food, cultural) of a young 3-year-old Asian child starting at nursery. Questions around race have always been debated from the perspective of their identity and relating to inclusion or exclusion of children. A child, parent/carer and a practitioner may be included or excluded depending on the attitudes and experiences of the people who are in a setting. The attitudes of young children towards difference are influenced by their experiences including the behaviour of adults in their home or in the setting.

Children in predominantly white areas struggled to accept black (non-white) children either by trying to place themselves away from these children or by declaring openly that they do not want to play with them because they may become dirty. On the other hand, an English child brought up in India realised the difference in skin colour, 'Why am I not the same colour as my friend – I was born in this country too?' Irrespective of their physical features, all children prefer to look like their friends and be respected and accepted (Targowska, 2001).

The notion of colour representing positive and negative aspects in a culture has been embedded in all countries. Representation of white as positive and black as negative has been a norm for several communities through generations. It has always been highlighted in children's literature, princes and princesses are illustrated with fair skin and positive roles and the negative, evil and disgraceful characters are portrayed in black colour. For example, angels are white and devils are black. However, there is evidence of raised awareness in contemporary children's literature that is depicting characters in a non-stereotypical way. The constant exposure to negative stereotypes from a wide range of sources, such as family, peers, films and media, may place a child in a dilemma and they may be tempted to emulate a close relative and use the same language and attitude. This attitude might pervade into several activities in the setting, for example, the role-play area, and the child might find it difficult to accept a different perspective from their peer or even a practitioner.

However, an adult in their role of a practitioner or a parent may already have been influenced by the stereotypes and may have impressions from their childhood resulting in their discrimination against children from families belonging to ethnic minority groups. Is this one of the prime reasons for a high rate of exclusions of children from ethnic minority groups? The highest rates of exclusions were found among Gypsy/Roma children, who were more than three times as likely to be excluded, followed by black Caribbean pupils. White, working-class pupils have serious problems in terms of underachievement, but black pupils remain three times more likely to be excluded than white. Several reports indicate that teachers had low expectations of black children (Maylor et al., 2009).

Is prejudice always experienced by people from ethnic minority groups and who are discriminated against by the majority groups? No, discrimination is reported from all over the world. Prejudice against ethnic minority groups has been prevalent in all the communities around the world. The hierarchy of power may be translated into how affluent families are considered to be powerful and how weak and disadvantaged families may be the victims of discrimination. However, globalisation has extended the borders and enabled people to travel inside and outside the country. This has led to relationships across borders and cultures, resulting in mixed heritage families.

Children of families with a mixed heritage are born in the UK with their parents belonging to different races or ethnic minority backgrounds. A major study reports 1 in 10 children are from mixed race families. Young people are six times more likely to be of mixed race than are adults. The proportion of children who face prejudices will increase in future generations and they will struggle to be accepted by both parents' communities as a result of not inheriting any specific physical features such as skin colour, hair colour or facial features that are prominently seen in others.

Do the resources used by the practitioners in early childhood promote inclusion or encourage children and their parents to feel included? Do the practitioners empower parents of children in their care to become involved in activities in the settings with children? Are practitioners from ethnic minority groups respected and valued?

What are the ways in which children are subject to prejudice and stereotyped because of their race? Parents and practitioners show racist attitudes and behaviour due to their prejudices and stereotypes. Children are influenced by their parents' and teachers' attitudes that are reflected as a result of their behaviour and use of negative language. Further lack of positive role models in their immediate environment may lead to negative perceptions of themselves. 'Children do not enter early childhood programs as empty slates but rather bring with them a myriad of perceptions of difference that they have taken up from their families, peers, the media and other social sources and negotiated in the representations of their own identities' (Robinson and Diaz, 2006: 4).

Milner (1983) reports that children pick positive and negative role perceptions towards different racial groups from a very early age. He suggests that children as young as 3 are aware of racial hierarchy 'in line with current adult practices' (ibid.: 122).

Early childhood practitioners may use a wide variety of resources that promote diversity in the setting in a positive way. This will benefit children and their families.

Theoretical base

Race is a contested and controversial term. People are categorised into specific groups on the basis of their skin colour and physical characteristics, with no scientific basis for this explanation. The Race Relations Act (1976) defines racial group as making references to race, colour, nationality, citizenship or ethnic or national origins (Jews, Sikhs, Romany Gypsies and Irish Travellers).

The first person to coin the term 'race' to connote categories of people was François Bernier in 1684 in his paper 'A New Division of the Earth' (Stuurman, 2000). For Bernier, race was referring to people who looked different physically being categorised as belonging to different races. Charles Darwin in *Descent of Man* (1874) argued that stronger races replace weaker races. European races were supposed to be superior to other races leading to colonisation of several countries around the world and oppressing the indigenous population in

Australia (Aboriginals), first nations (Canada) and Native Americans in America.

The concept of race is contested as socially constructed as opposed to being a biologically based label. So, in order to demonstrate this, race is sometimes presented in inverted commas.

Origins of racism – racism has been prevalent for the past 500 years all over the world. People are discriminated against by others on the basis of their colour, physical features, religion, culture, language, region and/or background.

At what age are children aware of their racial identity? Do children believe that they will belong to the same race when they grow older? Do children develop their stereotypes and prejudices from a very early age?

MacNaughton and Davis (p. 17) have cited this quote by Park (1928) illustrating the long history around debates on the issue of young children's racial awareness and identity:

> Racial consciousness, is ... as far as observation goes, an acquired trait, quite as much as the taste for olives or the mania for collecting stamps. Children do not have it. They take the world of human beings in which they find themselves as part of the order of nature and respond to a black or yellow face as readily as they do to a white, depending on the character and intimacy of the association. (Park, 1928: 16, cited in MacNaughton and Davis, 2009: 17)

Lasker challenged this notion that children are colour-blind and without 'race consciousness' in 1929. He suggested that children can form racial attitudes from a young age. Since then several studies have refuted Park's contention. Lasker argued that children's attitudes were formed by what adults taught them; their experiences of children's segregation on the basis of their race in addition to biased knowledge acquired from the curriculum shaped their knowledge of race.

Clark and Clark (1939), Criswell (1937, 1939) and Horowitz (1939) conducted early research on young children's 'racial' awareness and self-identification, examining the pre-school children's awareness of physical markers such as skin tone, hair colour and texture. One of the key findings of Clark and Clark (1939) was that children were aware of the racial differences at between 3 and 4 years of age.

Goodman (1964) mentioned that development of racial awareness occurs in three phases: phase 1 (2–3 years) children notice racial differences; phase 2 (4–5 years) children are able to express their orientation (positive and negative) towards specific racial groups; phase 3 (7–9 years) children express stereotypical and prejudiced attitudes.

Aboud and Skerry (1984) suggest that racial awareness begins at 4 years old and is able to relate to own group, awareness of being similar to own group, recognising being similar or dissimilar to others and being able to classify or label others based on their race.

Cognitive development theory described how children have an innate need to understand their world by sorting and classifying items around them and finding similarities and differences. Hirschfield (1995) referred to children using physical markers of 'race' (skin tone, facial feature and hair type) and to other characteristics (positive and negative) of 'race'.

In the UK children aged between 5 and 7 years of age were able to relate to their ethnic identity accurately (Davis et al., 2007). As children grow older, they are able to relate to social norms of racial prejudice being unacceptable. However, all children irrespective of their ethnic background were prone to show positive bias towards whiteness and negative bias towards blackness.

Social identity development theorists believe that children develop a sense of belonging to a specific group in three stages: (1) classification of people into different social groups, (2) differentiating the groups as having a positive or negative bias, and (3) developing their self-esteem based on the group to which they belong.

Ethnicity is often confused or is synonymously used with race. When referring to different groups of people who share common features (such as language, religion and culture) it is more appropriate to refer to people with different ethnicities rather than different races.

Critical race theory (CRT) originated in the 1970s in the USA and relates to racial reforms and deep-rooted racism. According to CRT, racism is deep-rooted in society and adopts a social constructionist approach to race. Delgado and Stefancic (2001: 162) believed 'CRT begins with a number of basic insights. One is that racism is normal, not aberrant in American society. Because racism is an ingrained feature of our landscape, it looks ordinary and natural to persons in the culture'. They further explain:

> Races are categories that society invents, manipulates, or retires when convenient. People with common origins share certain physical traits, of course such as skin colour, physique and hair texture … But these constitute only an extremely small portion of their genetic endowment, are dwarfed by that which

we have in common, and have little or nothing to do with distinctly human higher order traits such as personality, intelligence and moral behaviour. That society frequently chooses to ignore these scientific facts, creates races, and endows them with pseudo-permanent characteristics is of great interest to critical race theory. (Delgado and Stefancic, 2001: 7)

This theory emphasises the power of whiteness and that racism is permanent and embedded in education. However, CRT endeavours to make racism visible, as it is so entrenched in our society that it looks normal. Critical race theory encourages people of colour to articulate their experiences of racism in an explicit way.

Racial hierarchy – enlightened thinkers believed that all humans were considered to be equal, in principle; however, in practice society does not reflect this philosophy. Black and white are emotionally loaded concepts that are polarised. For example, white represents pure and good, and black has negative connotations. This also relates to skin colour of people which justifies people who are white to be powerful and those who are not white to be powerless, resulting in exclusion and disadvantage.

How do children develop racial awareness – are children 'colour-blind', leading them to be unaware of race and racism around them? Are children influenced by adults (parents and practitioners), media, resources (books, stories, displays) used in the early childhood settings?

Legislation

The legislation around race and inclusion has been presented from both the UK and international perspective. Race relations legislation makes it a duty to eliminate unlawful racial discrimination and to promote equality and good relations between people of different racial groups. All early years settings will have developed an equal opportunity policy that will enable all the staff employed in the early childhood setting to adhere to the policy.

The Race Relations Act 1976 defines a racial group by its race, colour, nationality, citizenship or ethnic or national origins (Jews, Sikhs, Romany Gypsies and Irish Travellers are covered, among others). The Race Relations Act 1976 and amended version in 2000 makes it unlawful to discriminate against anyone on the grounds of their race, colour, nationality, religious beliefs and national or ethnic origins.

However, all the legislation around discrimination has been covered by new legislation: the Equality Act 2010 that came into force in October 2010. All settings have responsibility and an obligation not to discriminate against people with a 'protected characteristic' under previous equality legislation. Race is constructed as one of the protected characteristics of the Equality Act 2010. The Equality Act 2010 (DfE, 2010) is a single legal framework that tackles disadvantage and discrimination from different perspectives. Single equality laws around race, disability and gender were combined under the equality law in 2010 to reduce bureaucracy. This change was effective from April 2011. Early childhood settings are not allowed to unlawfully discriminate based on race and ethnicity. This is applicable to children, their parents or carers, as well as practitioners.

The United Nations Convention on the Rights of Children 1989 (UNCRC) was an international agreement that was ratified by the UK in 1991. The UN convention includes a series of articles that describes the rights of children and young people up to age 18 years. The UNCRC articles challenge discrimination relevant to race. These are Articles 2, 14, 20 and 30 that recommend that the government should ensure all children can access their rights and challenge discrimination of children's rights and opportunities based on their race and religion.

> Article 2: Children must be treated without discrimination of any kind irrespective of the child's or his or her parent's or legal guardian's race, colour, sex, language, religion, political or other opinion, national, ethnic or social origin, property, disability, birth or other status.

> Article 14: Children have the right, according to their capacities, to form and express views and to have freedom of thought, conscience and religion.

> Article 20: Children who cannot be looked after by their own family must be looked after properly, by people who respect their religion, culture and language.

> Article 30: Children of ethnic, religious or linguistic minorities shall not be denied the right to enjoy their own culture, religion or language.

The Children Act 2004 places a duty on services to ensure that every child, whatever their background or circumstances, has the support they need to achieve the five Every Child Matters (ECM) outcomes (DfES, 2003).

The Early Years Foundation Stage (EYFS) is a statutory framework

(DCSF, 2008b). All settings providing access to learning, development and care of children from birth to 5 are required to follow EYFS. 'Inclusive practice' is one of the commitments to the EYFS principle of 'A unique child'. This refers to children's entitlements – their right be treated fairly regardless of race, religion or abilities. The EYFS states explicitly – both within its statutory requirements and guidance – that no child should be disadvantaged by their ethnicity, culture or religion, home language, family background, disability, special educational needs, gender or ability. 'All children, irrespective of ethnicity, culture or religion, home language, family background, learning difficulties or disabilities, gender or ability should have the opportunity to experience a challenging and enjoyable programme of learning and development' (EYFS).

Government initiatives

Building Futures: Believing in Children – a focus on provision for black children in the Early Years Foundation Stage – provides additional guidance for settings on how to include children from Black African and Black Caribbean heritage or any mixed black background. Practitioners are encouraged to reflect on their prejudices and challenge attitudes, and endeavour to provide quality provision.

Black History Month (BHM) or African History Month (AHM) is celebrated to commemorate significant events and notable people in black history. This is held every October in Britain and February in USA and Canada. During this month, knowledge of black history and cultural heritage is promoted to raise awareness and disseminate information on positive contributions of black people to these societies.

Tickell (2011) reviewed EYFS and made strong recommendations based on the feedback from the practitioners to retain key elements of EYFS, especially 'Unique child' endorsing the inclusiveness of the foundation stage curriculum.

Examples of good practice

Mac Naughton and Davis (2009) believe that 'developing anti-racist pedagogies requires educators to locate and name the effects and implications of "race" in children's lives and in their own lives'. So, it is essential for an early childhood setting to explore the concept of race from a child and an adult's perspective.

Case study

Every Friday during circle time, all children are allowed to ask a question followed by discussion with rest of the group. A 3½-year-old child asked the practitioner, who is from an ethnic minority group: 'Why do you look different? Why is your skin dark?' The practitioner asked all the children: 'I am different because I am special. Wouldn't it be boring if everybody looked the same?' All the children agreed. Another boy commented: 'My hair is curly; your hair is straight.' After several other comments from other children, the practitioner asked another question: 'What cake did you have for your birthday last week?' The girl excitedly replied, 'OOOH, I had a beautiful chocolate cake with Dora the Explorer on the cake!!!!'

Other excited children joined in claiming to love chocolate cake. The practitioner then explained that as there are different types of cakes – chocolate cake, cream cake and so on – that have different colours, so there are people with different skin colours. But, irrespective of different skin colours, everybody is a human being and 'loves different types of cakes'. This led to more discussion, when children started to compare their skin colour, hair colour, with tan, with spots, without spots, and so on.

Settings must:

1. Offer a rich learning environment in which all children and their families feel welcome, respected and valued. This should include establishing opportunities for all parents to communicate their child's needs to the practitioners; and ensuring practitioners have the knowledge and understanding to support children to freely explore their culture, heritage and faith without feeling stigmatised or self-conscious.

2. Use appropriate resources to raise awareness of differences in culture, religion, background, circumstances and issues that may lead to exclusion of children due to prejudice or discrimination.

3. Challenge stereotypical attitudes and change attitudes of practitioners and parents. Adults may prefer to isolate and exclude themselves from the mainstream and avoid being proactive rather than be discriminated against and excluded. Settings must endeavour to understand the needs of children and their families, so that every family experiences the setting as inclusive.

In order to enable inclusion, early childhood settings and schools should:

• Be committed to inclusion by having a named member of staff (named equality co-ordinator or inclusion co-ordinator) responsible for race equality.

- Provide a welcoming environment with approachable staff enabling all families to access the setting.

- Have accurate information about all the children in the setting, such as ethnicity, religion and naming systems. Be aware of how to spell and pronounce names correctly.

- Identify the need for training around race irrespective of the ethnic make-up of the setting and surrounding areas.

- Encourage practitioners to gain confidence to challenge orthodox practices and attitudes that are discriminatory. Ensure all staff employed in the setting are able to access training to raise their awareness of diversity.

- Ensure all staff have a basic understanding and knowledge of faiths and cultures to ensure that everyone is catered for. Respond to children's questions on race and ethnicity honestly, sensitively and openly.

- Check that resources reflect cultural and ethnic diversity in a positive manner. For example, ensure dolls and puppets have accurate and realistic skin tones and facial features and that story books avoid portraying characters conforming to stereotypes. Show and tell activity – all children and members of their families can be given opportunities to share their resources and culture with other children and the practitioners in the setting.

 Case study

Colour-blind or colour aware?

Ben, a 4-year-old boy in an early childhood setting in Manchester, was found scrubbing his hands vigorously, by an early childhood practitioner. When Ben was asked the reason for scrubbing, he replied saying that he was cleaning himself properly so that he can be clean and white like other children.

A white child but different from majority

Another 4-year-old child living in India with his white British parents, ran into his house screaming 'Mum, why am I not brown in colour and not like my friends Nitin, Ravi and Manish, although I was born in India like them?'.

Challenging children's ideas

A 4-year-old boy tried to clarify his ideas with an Indian visitor.

Continues

Continued

> Child: Are you Indian?
>
> Visitor: Yes, I am.
>
> Child with quizzical face: Are all Indians violent?
>
> Visitor: No, not really, why?
>
> Child: I saw this film with my mum and dad. They showed Indians using bows and arrows. My dad said all Indians are violent.
>
> Visitor: They are not violent. Indians use bows and arrows to protect themselves. There are two types of people who are called Indians: Native Americans who live in America and those who are from India.

Some reflections

- Children are aware of the differences irrespective of where they live.

- It is important to challenge children's views, especially if they are discriminatory, and clarify the ideas in a sensitive manner.

- Children and their parents should be provided with opportunities to raise their awareness of children from different races and their characteristics in a positive manner.

As a practitioner and parent how would you respond to empower and enable these children to accept their skin colour and be proud of their background?

Think tank – inclusion is not being tokenistic:

> A setting may claim their inclusiveness by displaying posters with people from different races displayed on the walls in the classrooms or corridors. Unless these posters are discussed by the practitioners with the children with questions such as why are these people different to each other, where do they come from, what might the background of these people be, and so on, children may not make any sense of these posters. These discussions may encourage children to understand the posters and relate to anybody from their acquaintances, friends or from the media or literature.

Metaphors

Melting pot versus a salad bowl – these metaphors have been used to compare how settings accepted people (children and their families) as in a melting pot, whereby everyone was mixed together to become one single product, expecting all to conform with the majority. Salad bowl, which is considered to be a better metaphor, refers to different vegetables of different colours, tastes, textures and flavours mixed together in a large bowl which will look attractive and colourful, retaining its original character of individual vegetables.

This is reflected in a popular poem titled 'British' by Benjamin Zephaniah. In this poem Zephaniah refers to all the people from different countries entering into Britain who are assimilated into the melting pot of British society. He is comparing British society to a salad bowl. People from different cultures, races and ethnicities are encouraged to keep their culture alive and are not expected to give up their identities while becoming part of British society.

Debates and controversies

- We do not have any children from different races. Is that a good reason for practitioners not to raise awareness of children about diversity? Children would benefit from being aware of differences and learn to be tolerant and accepting in their later life. So, settings must provide opportunities to extend knowledge and understanding about different races and their backgrounds.

- Who am I? What issues might impact the children, their parents and early childhood practitioners who are from ethnic minority groups? Several young children from ethnic minority groups are confused about their identity, so they may attempt to be like the majority children irrespective of geographical location.

- Are black and ethnic minority groups a homogenous group? How are they different?

- How much training can practitioners receive to raise their awareness about the ethnic minority groups?

- Is it possible for a practitioner to be realistic in including children and their families from different minority groups? Is inclusion tokenistic? Is training provided to practitioners on meeting the diverse needs of children and their families belonging to different races and ethnic minority groups?

- Do positive black role models (for example, Barack Obama, President of the USA) significantly impact on the self-esteem of children from ethnic minority groups?

- Who is superior? Do children believe that specific groups of children are more able and confident, which becomes a self-fulfilling prophecy?

• Are practitioners from different minority groups encouraged to participate in the recruitment process? Do employers publicise their recruitment campaign to a wider society, enabling practitioners from diverse communities to apply for jobs and make the recruitment process fair?

 Discussion point

How do settings ensure children are provided with positive role models through resources in the role-play area, books and stories, displays, games and toys and inviting guest speakers from different countries and cultures? How would you ensure these resources are not used in a tokenistic manner?

Implications

Early childhood settings must ensure they promote positive attitudes to differences between people and enable children to unlearn any negative attitudes. This is to ensure feelings of superiority among white children and inferiority among children from ethnic minorities are tackled. Settings need to be familiar with the need to understand the concept of racism, and encourage early childhood practitioners to access training to understand racism and its implications for children and their families. They should ensure staff of early childhood settings are provided with opportunities to discuss issues around racism in an open forum and honestly.

Children

• When children are valued and respected they develop positive self-identity and develop to their potential.
• When young children are exposed to children from diverse families, raising their awareness, they learn to respect and celebrate difference from an early age.
• A wide range of resources that portray positive images of children belonging to all races needs to be used to create awareness.
• Provide opportunities for children to express themselves without any inhibitions, and involve them in resolving any issues sensitively.

Parents

• Access to services should be available for all parents, irrespective of their background or race.

- Parents and practitioners need to be able to respect and accept differences mutually.

- Parents can be involved in organising activities and in some decision-making in the setting.

- Parents should be encouraged to access settings. Settings should have an open-door policy encouraging parents to share their culture – unique ways of celebrating festivals, recipes, antiques, stories from the past (especially from grandparents), and so on.

Practitioners

- Recruitment of practitioners from different minority groups will raise the profile of the setting.

- Raise awareness about the needs of children and their families from different ethnic minority groups.

- Provide training to create awareness and develop positive attitudes towards people from different races.

- Use a sensitive approach as well as an open mind (without making assumptions) while communicating with parents.

- Political correctness may force early childhood settings to acquire appropriate resources, however, practitioners need to ensure the resources are used in such a way that children learn to accept and respect differences.

 Research issues

The key areas explored to research inclusion from the perspective of race can include:

- Awareness of racial differences in children.
- Children's perception of their identity.
- Strategies used by practitioner to include children from different races.
- Attitudes of children and their parents/carers towards black practitioners.
- Resources used to raise awareness of race.
- Strategies used to involve parent of children from ethnic minority families.
- Practitioner's attitude to education and achievement of children from ethnic minority families.

Continues

Continued

- Explore stereotypes embedded in children, parents and practitioners around race in the current context.

The self devaluation study by Clark and Clark (1939) is one of the key researches that have been conducted to see the impact on young children of the shift in the political ideologies as well as raised awareness due to the presence of positive role models. They reported that children as young as 3 are aware of racial differences. They conducted an experiment with 253 African American children where they presented four dolls (two brown with black hair and two white with yellow hair). These children were asked questions about colour and identity. When asked to hand in the doll of a specific colour more than 90 per cent of the children identified the doll's colour appropriately. When asked if the doll resembled an African American child or a white child, again the choice of more than 90 per cent was accurate. However when asked to hand in a doll that looked like themselves, 66 per cent picked a brown doll while the rest chose a white doll. When asked which doll looked best, which one was bad and which doll was the nicer colour, the results seem to indicate that they have devalued their racial identity. Sixty-six per cent referred to white dolls as best while 59 per cent described brown dolls as bad and 38 per cent believed brown dolls to be a nicer colour.

When this experiment was repeated with a much smaller sample (21 black children) 65 years later in the USA, by Davis (2005) using similar questions about a black and a white doll, 71 per cent of these children preferred the white doll – although the sample size is small, the results are significant. After the victory of Obama in the presidential elections, *Good Morning America* asked 19 black children aged 5–9 from Norfolk, Virginia, which doll did they like best and which doll looked most like them. Responses indicate that boys seem to prefer both or neither dolls and 88 per cent perceived that the black doll looked most like them. With regard to their preferences of dolls, 42 per cent liked playing with black dolls while a majority chose both. Some of the rationale for the results indicates that choice had little to do with race. It is worth noting that these children were older than those children in the original study. These choices could have been influenced by factors such as positive role models, the civil rights movement and more awareness of differences.

- What are the key findings of this research?
- List the strengths and limitations of this study.
- What is the relevance of this study in the UK and in the current context?
- How can you change this study using different methodology, using qualitative perspective?

Connolly et al. (2002) in 'Too young to notice?' studied 352 children aged 3–6 years from Northern Ireland in a survey. This report explored the cultural and political awareness of young children. The children were shown some common objects and photographs related to events and symbols related to Protestant and Catholic communities, and were asked whether they were aware of and understood their ethnic preferences, ethnic awareness, ethnic identity and ethnic prejudice. The children's responses were coded and statistically analysed. Children aged 3–6 years were aware of parades (49 per cent), flags (38 per cent), Irish dancing (31 per cent), conflict-related violence (21 per cent), football shirts (21 per cent), the terms Catholic and Protestant (7 per cent) and colours (5 per cent).

- What are the key findings of this research?
- Explore how your setting (employed or in placement) will include children from different backgrounds.
- List the strengths and limitations of this study.
- Can this study be repeated in a childcare setting in your area?

An unpublished small-scale study explored young children's perceptions around exclusion. Children aged around 3 and 4 years in the nursery class of a school were included in the discussion. Children were shown pictures of six children belonging to the same age range but to different backgrounds in relation to their race, gender, culture, ability, and so on. The children were told that in an imaginary situation, all these virtual children were going to join their group and they were instructed to pick one of the six children as their friend. Children started picking different children as their friend. It was realised by the researcher and the children that one of the six children was not chosen by any child in the group. As the last child declared his choice, all the children expressed their disappointment vociferously as a group for ignoring one of the six children. All the children were very conscious of the situation although it was an imaginary situation. Every child in the group wished and provided alternative solutions to ensure this child was included. Some of the solutions offered were 'Can we pick more than one friend?' or 'Everybody can take turns to befriend this child'. From this experience it is clear that children are aware of the implications of exclusion and illustrated feelings of empathy towards other children's feelings. This illustrates children's awareness of differences in addition to their eagerness to respect the differences. This small-scale project shows that children are aware and are able to empathise with a child being excluded, and this needs to be supported by adults with their positive role models and examples.

- What are the key findings of this research?
- Explore how your setting enables children to accept and respect each other.
- List the strengths and limitations of this study.
- Can this study be repeated in a childcare setting in your area?

Further reading

Gilborn, D. (2008) *Racism and Education: Coincidence and Conspiracy*. Abingdon: Routledge.

Lane, J. (2006) 'Some suggested information/resources that may be helpful in working for racial equality in the early years', www.childrenwebmag.com/articles/child-care-articles/racial-equality-information-for-early-years-workers.

Lane, J. (2008) *Young Children and Racial Justice: Taking Action for Racial Equality in the Early Years – Understanding the Past, Thinking about the Present, Planning for the Future*. London: National Children's Bureau.

MacNaughton, G.M. and Davis, K. (eds) (2009) *Race and Early Childhood Education: An International Approach to Identity, Politics, and Pedagogy*. New York: Palgrave Macmillan.

Robinson, K. and Diaz, C. (2006) *Diversity and Difference in Early Childhood Education: Issues for Theory and Practice*. Maidenhead: Open University Press.

Useful websites

Department for Education, http://www.education.gov.uk/.
Runnymede Trust, http://www.runnymedetrust.org/.
Pre-school Learning Alliance, http://www.pre-school.org.uk/.
Britkid, http://www.britkid.org/.

3

Culture and inclusion

Chapter overview

This chapter explores inclusion from the perspective of culture in the context of early childhood. The focus is on how the culture of a child or an adult (parents/carer of the child or early childhood practitioner) in an early childhood setting will influence or hinder inclusion.

What is culture? Does culture change from one generation to another? What are the reasons for the dynamic nature of culture? In modern society, multiculturalism is a norm owing to permeable boundaries between countries and regions. It is crucial for all children and adults to be proud of their backgrounds, traditions, beliefs and values. In the contemporary context, it is interesting to find out the preferences of individuals about their identity – British, English, Scottish, British Asian or British Asian (Chinese). Is there a significant difference between the cultures of English and Welsh families? Are young children able to relate to these differences? Does being in proximity, guarantee awareness of the differences in the cultures?

Self-identity is influenced by a range of factors – peers, curriculum, media, attitudes of practitioners, and so on. Is it globalisation that muddles up the individual's identity in relation to their nationality, region, ethnic identity and religion?

Society is becoming increasingly diverse and heterogeneous around the world. Britain has been found to be a popular destination for significant numbers of migrants from overseas, predominantly to study and work. The Office for National Statistics has reported that 48 per cent of the population increase is accounted for by migration (ONS, 2011b). In 2010, 11.4 per cent of the total UK population was born outside the UK.

What is culture?

Culture is a complex concept that has been interpreted and understood in different ways. Some of the concepts range from relating to attitudes, beliefs and values, to how festivals are celebrated, food, art, dresses, and so on. The following two definitions illustrate the different interpretations of culture.

> Culture can be a set of fundamental ideas, practices and experiences of a group of people that are symbolically transmitted generation to generation through a learning process. Culture may as well refer to the beliefs, norms, and attitudes that are used to guide our behaviours and solve problems. (Chen and Starosta, 1998: 25)

Siraj-Blatchford (1994: 28–9) points out, culture, like language, is dynamic and ever changing:

> Our parents pass on their culture to their children but they do it through vehicles such as language, play, art and literature. Schools and other educational institutions extend our learning in this way through humanities, science, the arts, etc. Our culture also determines what clothes we wear, our diet, religious beliefs and relationships. Culture is much more than this, but the important point is that it is learnt and that it is all around us.

Culture is a complicated phenomenon with several layers. Common knowledge of different cultures is superficial and is often perceived to relate to food, dress, language festivals, and so on. These symbols would differ from one family to another and would not be easily identifiable. The signs and symbols representing different cultures are concrete and explicit. When these symbols are exhibited, it is often considered as the main way of relating to other cultures. For example, a majority of the practitioners may display posters of different festivals in a childcare setting; however, there may be very little awareness about the context and background of different festivals. This may be due to a lack of knowledge and understanding of practitioners, especially with regard to the implicit and subconscious assumptions about beliefs, norms and attitudes of a culture. A larger chunk of the culture is abstract and implicit. It will be difficult for a person who does not belong to a culture to identify with certain customs and understand the values and beliefs of that culture from the outside.

Contexts of inclusion and exclusion

Children may be included or excluded unintentionally by children and adults, usually as a result of being unsure of the unknown and having inappropriate expectations. In the current climate, there is a lot of awareness (positive and negative) of multiculturalism from the media, television and the Internet. However, owing to superficial information, assumptions are based on the limited information available and may lead to individuals from different cultures being stereotyped and experiencing prejudice. Many immigrant families are entering the UK. The European Union opened up to East European countries and other countries due to deteriorating political situations: 'more than 100 million people arriving at the UK border and consider around 3.5 million applications to visit, live, work or study in the UK' (*UK Border Agency Business Plan April 2011–March 2015*).

The UK Home Office indicates that approximately 185,600 visas were granted to migrants, including Chinese, Indian, Pakistani, Russian, American, Taiwanese, Japanese and Nigerian, to study in the UK in 2011. These students may get a job and settle down in the UK. It is a common observation that a significant number of professionals (doctors and nurses) employed by the National Health Service (NHS) were born overseas. Families with young children entering the country are forced to access childcare when both parents are in employment and there is little support from, or often non-existent, extended family. So, these parents would require extended childcare to cover their long working hours. The expectations of all parents sending their children to an early childhood setting will be of high-quality care meeting their child's needs and holistic development irrespective of their different cultural backgrounds. So it is a huge responsibility on early childhood practitioners to ensure all children's needs are met appropriately, so that they can develop to their potential. Although the population of children in early childhood settings has been diverse, the composition of the childcare workforce has been predominantly white. Diversity in the cultures of children attending early childhood settings will challenge the practitioners' abilities and skills on how they would meet the diverse needs of children. Further, awareness of diversity at a young age enables children to empathise and respect people from other cultures.

Activity

Categorise the following aspects related to culture. Rate your knowledge and understanding according to the following:

A. I am familiar with this and am aware of the justification.

B. I know about this at a superficial level.

C. I do not know anything about this, not sure what it is.

Greetings – Hallo (Afrikaans), Hola (Spanish), Nei Ho (Cantonese), Hej (Danish), Bonjour (French), Dia Duit (Irish), shw mae (Southern Welsh).

Festivals – Rakhi (Hindu festival – this day is also known as Raksha Bandhan when a sister ties a piece of sacred thread around her brother's right wrist and has social significance), Baisakhi (Hindus and Sikhs celebrate as their new year), Hanukkah (Jewish festival of lights), Lent (period of 40 days, not including Sundays, leading up to Easter, the most important festival in the Christian calendar), Eid-ul-Adha (Islam 'Festival of Sacrifice'), Dussehra (Hindu festival that is celebrated by Hindus throughout the world at the same time, with varying rituals celebrating victory of good over evil).

Places of worship – gurudwara, temple, synagogue, church, Baha'i temple, mosque.

 Discussion point

- Values and beliefs – discuss how elders are greeted with respect, issues around cleanliness, how culture influences the way festivals are celebrated.

Give examples of how a popular festival such as Christmas is celebrated around the world. You might wish to add other aspects of your local culture.

Theoretical base

There are several theorists providing a wide range of perspectives on culture, such as Hall's (1976) cultural iceberg model, and Klug and Whitfield's (2003) model considering culture to be on a continuum from being traditional to being assimilated into the dominant culture. On a different spectrum, Trompenaars and Hampden-Turner (1998) developed a framework relating to cultural values around relationships with people, time and nature. Banks (2004) proposed five dimensions of multicultural education linking to curriculum.

Edward T. Hall's cultural iceberg model

Several practitioners believe that they are inclusive from the perspective of culture when they celebrate different festivals, display posters, and include a variety of dressing-up clothes from different cultures such as sarees, salwar kurtas in the role-play area. When a child questions what is the name of this dress, when and where do they wear these dresses and how to wear them, the practitioner is not sure.

Hall, an anthropologist, compared culture to an iceberg where there are some aspects visible and a large portion of culture is hidden beneath the water. The tip of the iceberg relates to explicit and concrete aspects of culture that are visible but the majority of the iceberg, which is invisible, is about beliefs, values and thought patterns influencing behaviour and is difficult to learn. From an early childhood context, it is important not only to learn ways of greeting (verbally and gestures), but also to understand the rationale behind it. This will be feasible when a practitioner not only asks a child to tell or find out from parents, but involves parents and or grandparents by inviting them into the setting to talk to the children, which may help them to internalise the information.

Is it possible for practitioners to become bicultural? Klug and Whitfield (2003) suggested that individuals – children and adults (parents and practitioners) – placed themselves on the continuum as traditional, bicultural and assimilated (modern) based on their experiences of diversity.

Bicultural children, family and practitioners can be classed as traditional as they have been strictly raised with their cultural norms and with minimum exposure to other cultures. Those children who are brought up by their grandparents may be traditional as a result of limited exposure to the dominant culture in addition to the values instilled from their own culture. A bicultural teacher or child may be aware of practices from both the cultures. They are able to switch comfortably between their own culture and the new culture. An assimilated person is one who has totally embraced the new cultural values and expectations. People who are categorised as assimilated are usually out of touch with their own culture. Physically, they may appear to be like an Asian or African in a British society but their values and attitudes may reflect the dominant culture's way of thinking. Individuals may not prefer to be identified as belonging to a minority community. It was also presumed that people belonging to the majority culture, and those with fair skin, were superior and may explain the reason for preferring to belong to the superior group. In African and Asian cultures, children and their families with fair skin may be given preferential treatment compared with the indigenous communities. Some children with dark skin may scrub themselves so hard assuming that their skin is dirty compared with some of their peers.

What about children from mixed marriages – would they adopt the dominant and superior culture? Are these children in any danger of being excluded from mainstream activities irrespective of their cultural orientation because of their appearance?

Influence of culture on values

Trompenaars and Hampden-Turner (1998) developed a framework that explains the implicit assumptions made about culture. They identify how cultural values relate to three issues – people, time and nature. Culture influences the way human beings treat each other. The way communities relate to people, time and nature is influenced by the values of different cultures. Some of the issues relevant to early childhood include the following.

Dependence or independence

A parent/practitioner or child may feel threatened about the amount of assistance provided to meet the needs of children, especially when it is expected and not available. Some cultural values may influence parents or practitioners to encourage children to be independent rather than being dependent. This may result in conflict in the opinions of parents and practitioners on how much support a child needs to receive – feeding, dressing, making decisions, and so on. This may be perceived differently in diverse cultures around the world.

Expression of emotions

The response of individuals to specific situations differs depending on the culture. Some cultures are neutral (mild expression), making use of understatements, and some are overt in their expression of emotions by being loud. Cultural orientation influences the tolerance of silence, tone, use of words and non-verbal communication such as eye contact, distance, touch and gesture. Lack of awareness may lead to poor communication and exclusion from mainstream activities. It is important for early childhood practitioners to be aware of the communication styles of children and their parents from different cultural backgrounds. It will be difficult to gain this knowledge from the parents, but observation and reflection will enable the practitioner to raise their awareness. However, it is crucial not to make assumptions based on the background of the child. Open communication between the practitioner and parents will resolve many problems that may occur as a result of misinterpretation or lack of communication.

Status

The status given to different professionals varies depending on their job, age, class, gender, profession or education. In addition, the elderly are given a lot of respect in some cultures. The respect is expected in the form of gestures, or how they are addressed. For example, in some cultures, the elderly are never addressed by their first names, especially by youngsters. Addressing another person by their first name would make some people uncomfortable and it may be even unacceptable. So, it is important for an early childhood practitioner to clarify with family members how they prefer to be addressed. In some south Asian cultures, elders would like to be addressed with respect in the form of well-mannered behaviour. Further, professionals such as doctors, lawyers, teachers, priests are given higher status.

Personal involvement

Some cultures tend to draw boundaries around relationships specific to individual contexts. Different cultures tend to maintain relationships outside the settings. It is important for a practitioner to be aware of specific or diverse orientation of individual families. Further formalities in the relationships may influence the manner in which relationships are maintained. For example, in some cultures, if an individual is celebrating an important occasion, he or she might like to invite people from other contexts, such as work, friends from school, college, neighbours and so on. It is common practice in Asian culture, especially in India, for wedding invitations to include the phrase – 'invite family and friends on the occasion of'.

Relationship with time

Some cultures have a different orientation to time. Cultures that value their past would consider certain traditions, relationship with ancestors and strong family ties important. Some cultures may find the present important, as the past is seen as unimportant and the future is unpredictable. People from certain cultures would see time slots and schedules to be important and lateness would cause great anxiety. On the other hand, some cultures perceive time to be a servant of people; punctuality is seen as a last priority and people are given high priority. In some cultures, parents would want their child to start attending an early childhood setting at a specific time and day that is considered to be auspicious, and would find certain times and days to be inauspicious. So they may not want their child to start on a day when other children start. Also, some parents may not attend their appointments at the scheduled time and might consistently be late. Awareness of parents' and practitioners' different orientations to time enables people to understand time management behaviours. It is crucial for parents to adapt to the mainstream culture.

It is essential that early childhood practitioners do not assume that all children and their families share values and beliefs that are similar to those embedded in the early childhood setting.

Relationship with nature

Some cultures have different orientations to nature. Some societies believe that nature can be controlled and some consider nature to be important and that human beings must abide by the forces of nature. In some western societies, technology dominates early childhood settings but in Scandinavian countries nature plays a bigger role.

Five dimensions of multicultural education

Banks (2004) has proposed five dimensions of multicultural education. The five dimensions include content integration, knowledge construction, prejudice reduction, equity pedagogy and empowering school culture and social structure.

1. Content integration relates to how the practitioner will integrate examples from diverse cultures to support the curriculum implemented in the early childhood setting. This can be illustrated by the use of a range of resources such as music, books, puppets, the home corner and games representing different cultures. Parents and grandparents can be involved to contribute to planning and implementing a rich and diverse curriculum.

2. Knowledge construction: Banks (2004) suggests four levels of knowledge construction. The first is the contribution approach. Practitioners must acknowledge people from different cultures who can make a significant impact and must be integrated into the curriculum. The second level is the additive approach. This approach refers to when a specific concept is related to different cultures. For

example, when discussing festivals, the practitioner can discuss different festivals celebrated by children in the setting. The third level is the transformation level. In this level the practitioner should ensure the information used is appropriate to the age and development stage of children. The practitioner should encourage all children to share their general day-to-day experiences with others in the room and the setting, if appropriate. The final level is social action approach. This level requires that the students implement what they have learned in the previous levels. A social action approach relates to developing critical thinking skills. This has been criticised as not relevant at the early childhood stage.

3. Prejudice reduction focuses on how the setting and its staff can reduce racial stereotypes and increase democratic attitudes, values and behaviour. A range of strategies are used by practitioners to change the attitudes of children by using multicultural resources as well as recruiting staff from diverse backgrounds.

4. Equity pedagogy refers to ways in which the academic abilities of children from diverse backgrounds and cultures could be improved by using appropriate teaching and learning styles. Practitioners could use stories, art and music, as well as creative play, to stimulate learning.

5. Empowering school culture and social structure focuses on a holistic approach promoting participation interactions between the staff and students as well as achievement levels of children from different backgrounds.

Early childhood practitioners should be able to implement Banks's five dimensions of multicultural education even at early childhood level as children must be encouraged to be aware of diversity and accept and respect the differences. It is crucial that the practitioners and the settings have the right attitude to ensure diverse cultures are promoted positively.

Legislation

The key influencing legislation is at global, national and the setting levels. All settings are expected to ensure they provide opportunities for children to access all legislation.

Global level

The UNCRC has granted all children a comprehensive set of rights that has been signed and ratified by the UK government. Some of the articles that relate to culture include:

Article 2: the Convention applies to everyone whatever their race, religion, abilities, whatever they think or say, no matter what type of family they come from.

Article 14: you have the right to think and believe what you want and to practise your religion, as long as you are not stopping other people from enjoying their rights. Parents should guide children on these matters.

Article 30: you have a right to learn and use the language and customs of your family, whether or not these are shared by the majority of the people in the country where you live.

National level

At national level, there is legislation and guidance that impact on children. These are the Equality Act 2010 and the EYFS as a framework for all early childhood settings to deliver good quality services to all children in England. At the national level all early childhood settings registered with OFSTED are required to implement EYFS as a framework to ensure that their provision meets the learning and development requirements for all children. All early childhood settings are required to comply with the welfare regulations, in section 40 of the Childcare Act 2006.

One of the key purpose and aims of the EYFS statutory framework is: 'All children, irrespective of ethnicity, culture or religion, home language, family background, learning difficulties or disabilities, gender or ability have the opportunity to experience a challenging and enjoyable programme of learning and development' (DCSF, 2008b: 5).

The EYFS comprises four themes. Under the theme 'Unique child', the second principle refers to inclusive practice. One of the commitments is titled 'Equality and diversity'. Two of the statements under the Theme 1.2 Equality and Diversity are relevant specifically to all children irrespective of their culture.

The EYFS states: 'All children are entitled to enjoy a full life in conditions which will help them take part in society and develop as an individual, with their own cultural and spiritual beliefs.' 'Practitioners [must] ensure that their own knowledge about different cultural groups is up-to-date and consider their own attitudes to people who are different from themselves' (DCSF, 2008b, Theme 1.2 Equality and Diversity).

The EYFS has been reviewed by Tickell and a revised simpler framework was published in March 2012 (DfE, 2012). One of the new areas of learning is 'Understanding the world' that relates to learning about cultures and beliefs, and has replaced 'knowledge and understanding of the world'.

Every Child Matters (ECM) (DfES, 2003b) has been a significant government policy that supports inclusion. The five outcomes of children, met by the settings, improve children's lives. However, there has been a slight shift in the terminology, and the position of ECM in the current Coalition government is not clear.

The Equality Act 2010 has replaced all existing equality legislation relating to discrimination of children and adults – parents and practitioners. This Act recommends that all early childhood settings ensure they regularly review practices, policies and procedures. This will guarantee people with a 'protected characteristic' who should not be discriminated against.

At the early childhood setting level, practitioners have to ensure they implement all the guidelines recommended by the government. It is the responsibility of the setting to ensure they review the policies regularly to reflect the changes made by the government. All settings develop their policies to promote equal opportunities for all children. These policies are reviewed periodically and updated.

Examples of good practice

'A multi-cultural curriculum [will exist when] it is accepted by all sections of society that to draw on a diversity of cultural sources, and to incorporate a world perspective, was proper and unremarkable' (Swann Report, 1985: 324). The positive tone of this quote might sound like a distant dream. Although this insight is more than 25 years old, it is still relevant in the contemporary context.

The early childhood population is becoming more diverse and it is crucial for early childhood practitioners to embed multiculturalism reflecting diverse cultures in the settings. An early childhood practitioner should endeavour to build their knowledge and understanding of individual children and their families rather than base them on stereotypes. This will enable children to be aware of the differences from an early age and accept and respect differences. Lane (2008) cites Parekh (2005) who believes:

> Multiculturalism is not about safeguarding self contained ethnic and cultural boxes but rather about intercultural fusion in which a culture freely borrows bits of others and creatively transforms both itself and them. Far from implying that each individual should remain rooted in his or her own culture and flit between them, multiculturalism

Continues

Continued

> requires that they should open themselves up to the influence of others and engage in a reflective and sometimes life enhancing dialogue with others. (Lane, p. 142–3)

Lane clearly advocates practitioners to be open and flexible and embrace other cultures in addition to respecting their own culture.

Promote multicultural awareness and self-esteem through the concept of 'Around the World'. Children can make their own passports by folding and stapling 10 sheets of white paper. They can explore three countries by searching on a globe for the location of each country, explaining how to travel to this country, the food eaten and the dress worn, and so on.

Children can prepare their tour of these countries at specific times of the year to coincide with some important event, for example, a festival or national days. Children can research the flag of the country and the location of the country. For every country visited, the children wear a prop from that country. Take pictures of each child wearing his or her hat or prop and glue the pictures into each child's individual passport and give it to them along with a 'world traveller' certificate at the end of the year. This project will involve acquiring several development skills.

Bulletin board: symbols, photographs and pictures from different religions and cultures can be used to create a bulletin board with this multicultural activity. Discuss the symbols with regard to their significance and in which context they are used, places where these symbols are displayed. Again the complexity of the symbols and information displayed on the bulletin board can vary according to the age of the child.

I am different – children in the group can explore how they are different from each other. They could use physical characteristics such as skin colour, eye colour, hair colour, height, etc.

Multicultural book – children can be involved in preparing a scrapbook with photographs of children from different parts of the world Young children can also dictate their thoughts about the pictures to you. Use Persona Dolls to discuss different attributes of children.

Celebrate multicultural day once a month – include music, food, art and craft activities from different parts of the world as well as Britain. Display some real objects used by children at home, for example dresses, jewellery, cutlery, books and music, that are different to those used in the setting. Play music from different countries.

Encourage grandparents and/or elderly relatives of children to visit the setting. This will enable a bond to be cultivated between the two generations. They can relate stories, sing songs, discuss games that they used to play. This activity not only develops bonds between two generations but also provides an opportunity to revive forgotten culture from the past. This day could be celebrated as grandparents' day.

Use the notice board to provide information about newly arrived families in the setting. Practitioners should build strong relationships with the carers of children by displaying brief information about the child, family's background and a family photograph. This will enable practitioners to gain greater insight into the lives of the children they will care for. Photographs of staff working in the setting would help the parents to relate to the practitioners.

It is important for a practitioner to ensure they pronounce children's names in their setting appropriately. The practitioner can be from the local area or may be an immigrant who is from a different country. So it is crucial for any practitioner to clarify background information before making assumptions. The following questions may be asked:

• How do you pronounce your name?

• Which languages do you speak at home?

• Do you know any songs or stories in your languages?

• What special days do you celebrate at home?

• Do you wear any special clothes at home or during festivals or when you visit your grandparents?

• What food do you eat at home and how do you eat?

Food for thought

As an early childhood practitioner, how would you ensure information is accessible to all children and their families?

Discuss with children during circle time, 'What if all children were alike?'

Celebrate international mother-tongue day (UNESCO) on 21 February.

Display a special welcome board with the word 'Welcome' in several languages spoken by children in the setting and at home.

Celebrate birthdays and festivals as children would celebrate traditionally in their homes.

What is in a name?

It is important for an individual to be called by their name appropriately. Some of the children belonging to different cultures with 'unusual' names, might be called by a shortened name as it will be convenient or they may not be able to pronounce their full name properly. Some children prefer to conform to British naming patterns and shorten their name or take an Anglicised name to be accepted by their peers. Zealey (1995) collated a wide range of naming patterns around the world and presented background information on the rationale. An understanding of the naming patterns will enable the early childhood practitioner to relate to the names of children in an appropriate manner.

Significance of names and surnames

In some cultures, names often have religious or cultural connotations. It has been acknowledged by several people belonging to different cultures that they cannot fit their names around the British system of recording first or Christian names, surnames and middle names due to discrepancies in their naming patterns as discussed later.

It is always good practice not to make any assumptions about the family names as people in second marriages, in step-families and unmarried women may prefer to give their surnames to their children. Practitioners may find it useful to discuss with a family member how to pronounce a child's name and to understand the naming pattern. Basic information on different naming patterns from different regions of the world are summarised below.

European naming pattern
Naming patterns vary in different parts of Europe. The majority of children inherit their father's surname. It is common practice for some children to take both their mother's and father's surnames. In some Scandinavian countries, the surnames might change from sons to daughters. For example, in Iceland, Gunnar Olafson might call his son Peter Gunnarson and his daughter Ella Gunnarsdottir.

Muslim naming patterns
Children may be given one of 99 names of Allah which is attached to the personal name. Religious names come first, not the personal names. When a child attends a nursery, the practitioners might assume that the first name may be the preferred name and may start addressing the child with the first name, and this may be inappropriate from the religious perspective. Many women may have titles given such as Bibi, Begum and Khatoon. This title is different to her surname. So it may be necessary to clarify with the parent how they should be addressed.

Sikh naming patterns
Naming patterns will be similar for males and females. A boy and a girl might be given a similar name, for example, Manjit. The titles might be different for males and females. Males could be given Singh (lion) and females could be called Kaur (princess). So, a first name might not indicate the gender of the child, unless the practitioner is

aware of the title following the first names, 'Singh' or 'Kaur'. A woman's title might change after marriage.

Indian (Hindu) naming patterns

There are many differences in the naming patterns of children from India. Most of the names have meanings. Traditionally, boys are named after gods and girls are named after goddesses who might be family deities. The names may end with second names – Kumar (male) or Kumari (female) – that may be different from the surname. Another region refers to Bhai (meaning brother) for all males and Behn (sister) for females as part of their names. Some families, for example from the South Indian state of Tamil Nadu, will give their children their father's first name as their surname. Some families may like to add their occupational status to the names of children in addition to the surnames. Families from another region like to add to the name, the child's grandfather's first name and some of their favourite gods' names too. This might result in five or six given names in addition to the surname and first name. Naming patterns differ from one region to another.

African naming patterns

The names of children from African families tell a story about the child, family and society. The naming patterns differ from one ethnic group to another. Children may be named after their birth order in the family or the circumstances in which the baby is born (during war, while travelling, or born following prayers).

Chinese naming patterns

Names of individuals of Chinese origin will consist of three components as in British naming patterns – first, middle and surname – but in reverse order. All girls and boys may have a similar middle name (Thi and Ven) respectively. Several children of Chinese origin will have an Anglicised name for the sake of convenience. A Chinese woman may not formally change her surname after marriage, although by custom she may add her husband's surname to her maiden name.

Role of parents and practitioners

It is important for a practitioner to get all the names of the child right.

Parents might suggest the preferred name with the child's approval.

Clarify the names of both parents, as wives may not share the same name as their husbands.

Make no assumptions, and clarify the surnames of children and both their parents.

Practitioners should make an effort to comprehend the ways in which the child's names are spelt and pronounced appropriately. It is also important to understand the order of the names.

Clarify the names of children and their surnames, and the marital status of parents.

Practitioners should not make assumptions about the surnames. The surnames of children might be different from those of their mothers for several reasons. In the modern context women may prefer to retain their maiden name and not necessarily change their surnames after getting married.

 ## Case study

Razia is the manager of a nursery in Yorkshire. The town has a predominantly white population. The nursery is attended mainly by children from white British families. A majority of the staff in the setting are also white, apart from the manager.

The setting was recently awarded an outstanding grade in the inspection by OFSTED, flagging its unique inclusive practice. The setting values the uniqueness of children, their families and all staff in the setting, and capitalises on the strengths of everybody in the setting and respects everybody as an individual with strengths and weaknesses. All staff members are included in decision-making. The practitioners have decided to introduce something 'new' in the setting to the children every week. For example, it could be a nursery rhyme from another country, craft, skills, a word from another language, celebrating Christmas in a different style (Russian), a gesture, or finding out about a custom or ritual from another culture. The settings strive not only to include world culture but also to emphasise and encourage aspects of local culture which may have been taken for granted.

Children and their families are encouraged to contribute to a 'dynamic culture' box. Children and practitioners take pride in making their contributions. So they discuss with friends and family (national and international) as well as use the Internet to gather their ideas. Planning meetings include all staff members in the setting to decide what to use from the 'dynamic culture' box in the month and reflected on it the following month. Razia, as the manager, strongly believes in inclusion and has facilitated inclusion in the setting by encouraging everybody to contribute and ensuring inclusion is not superficial or tokenistic.

Is the practice in this setting realistic or idealistic?

Do you think 'dynamic culture' box will work in your setting?

How would you adapt this idea to suit your setting?

What is inclusion?

Inclusion is not about:

- Admitting children from different countries and cultures to raise the profile of the setting.
- Ensuring Id, Diwali and Chinese New Year are celebrated every year.
- Displaying a welcome poster in different languages.
- Having multicultural dolls.
- Having story books from different countries on the bookshelf.

What is inclusion about?

Inclusion is about:

Celebrating different festivals and also ensuring the local culture is not marginalised or neglected.

Raising awareness about how Diwali, Id, Chinese New Year and Christmas are celebrated in different countries – including those children in the school as well who would celebrate these festivals.

Displaying a welcome poster in different languages could be extended to – how many languages are we aware of, where are these languages spoken, how does this language sound, does this language have a script?

Using multicultural dolls creatively to raise awareness about different cultures. Staff can stimulate children to think of names of boys and girls in their cultures/countries. Where do these dolls come from? What costumes do these children and adults from specific countries wear on special occasions?

Finding out where these stories come from. Where is this country on the world map?

Is the storyline similar or different to stories from your own country? How are the characters in this story depicted – any stereotypes or prejudices implied?

 Activity

What do we know about different festivals celebrated in the setting? Pick two festivals celebrated by Christians, Muslims, Jews and Hindus and discuss the following:

- Name of festival.
- Who celebrates this festival.
- Any traditions linked to the festival.
- Any differences in how this festival is celebrated.
- Significance (why this festival is celebrated).

Influence of culture on child-rearing practices

Culture influences parents' beliefs and practices about child-rearing and children's development. The child-rearing practices of the West are characterised as 'individualistic' leading to competence and independence. On the other hand, non-western and non-industrialised societies are more traditional and driven by collective goals, participation in collective events, obedience to authority and developing altruistic orientation (Rosenthal, 2000). Families from Asian, African and South American countries that migrated to western and industrialised countries such as the UK, the USA, Australia and in Europe are considered to be culturally diverse with different beliefs and values in relation to child-rearing practices.

Child-rearing practices vary in different cultures. Harkness and Super (1992) developed the term 'parental ethno theories', which refers to the experience of daily routines that parents have with their children which are influenced by the cultural experience of the immediate community. These influence child-rearing practices, such as feeding schedules and sleeping routines. When culture is mentioned, assumptions have been based on the fact that all the child-rearing practices are almost alike in all western and industrialised countries.

Early childhood practitioners should have a broader perspective of, and be open to accept, different childcare practices. Confusion and contradiction of child-rearing practices between parent(s) and early childhood settings may lead to disagreements. Conflicts occur between parents and carers over issues such as changing nappies, feeding, comforting, toilet-training and educating babies. It is crucial for practitioners to reduce prejudices based on ethnically diverse families, and support tolerance of and become comfortable with diverse childcare practices. This can be enabled by clear communication between early childhood practitioners.

Debates and controversies

Do settings create a balance of home culture as well as diverse cultures around the world? To find the right balance between the local culture and other cultures, ensure that the local culture is not marginalised and too much emphasis is not put on other cultures. The feasibility of including all children appropriately might be complicated. Settings should not sideline the dominant culture in an attempt to demonstrate their inclusive practice. Are children able to conform to mainstream culture without losing their own culture?

Can a practitioner be open and be able to consider their own prejudices and assumptions and avoid judging the skills and abilities of children, parents or carers based on stereotypes? What opportunities are provided for practitioners to reflect on their practices? Whose practices, values and beliefs are right – practitioners' or parents'? Disagreements and conflicts between practitioners and parents may lead to resentment.

Practitioners may overlook ethnic diversity in the community. This may reflect on the range of resources available in the early childhood setting. Lindon comments:

> There is always some ethnic diversity in a neighbourhood, although large urban areas are likely to have populations with more obvious differences in skin colour, physical appearance and dress. It would be poor practice to restrict play resources in a mainly white area on the grounds that 'nobody round here looks like that'. (Lindon, n.d.)

Is it possible to find qualified people from different cultures to recruit as early childhood practitioners to reflect the diversity of children in the setting? The main issue relates to attracting people as a result of low pay and status of early childhood practitioners in the community.

Implications for practice

Ensure the setting reflects a wide range of resources portraying the cultural diversity of the setting as well as the community. The resources must be actively used by the practitioners rather than just displayed on the walls. Ensure all areas in the setting consist of multicultural resources such as books, art and craft, costumes in the role-play area, artefacts, music heard from different languages and countries, food ingredients from different countries, posters depicting important festivals or events related to different cultures.

Display positive implementation of policy to promote inclusive practice. Settings' policies should reflect the diverse population of the setting, including children and practitioners. Encourage the participation of all staff members in developing an equal opportunities policy addressing diverse population in early childhood settings so that everybody takes ownership of the policy and implements it appropriately.

Settings must ensure culture is embedded in routine activities rather than from a tokenistic perspective. Provide choice for all children to develop their self-identity by encouraging their family and/or community to share their cultural experiences with the practitioner and other children in the setting. The involvement of extended families will provide opportunities for children to explore different cultures.

This will empower children to develop positive self-esteem and be proud of their cultural background. Encourage children and adults to be firmly rooted in their own culture and or bicultural. Practitioners must make sure they do not provide any spoken or unspoken messages that the mainstream culture is superior to their home culture. If the right balance is not found in the setting, a child will be forced to choose mainstream culture and give up their own (minority) culture.

Intervene to challenge in a sensitive manner when children are demonstrating stereotypical behaviour or language. Teach children to be critical thinkers, especially with regard to prejudice and stereotype. Encourage critical thinking by examining and questioning. For example, how would you feel when you were prejudiced?

Organise formal and informal training to share good practice in relation to appropriate use of resources, learn about cultures and implement equal opportunities policies. Invite people from a wide range of backgrounds and cultures, professionals working in different organisations promoting culture and arts, academics who have conducted research into inclusion and culture. Undergraduate courses should integrate issues around diversity and culture in the curriculum that will enable students to enhance their knowledge and understanding.

Research Issues

This section refers to research published on some significant issues to do with culture. Some issues to consider for research include:

- How does inclusive practice of a setting enable children to develop their self-identity?
- Children's knowledge and understanding of their culture.
- Awareness of diversity in young children in the foundation stage.
- Awareness of multiculturalism in early years practitioners.
- Good practice around inclusion of children from different cultures.
- What are the differences in perceptions about childcare between practitioners and parents?

- Expectations of parents from different ethnic minority groups regarding the children.
- Factors influencing practitioners' knowledge and understanding of cultural practices of children.
- Strategies used to raise awareness of different cultures in an early childhood setting.

A brief summary of each research document is followed by questions that will stimulate thinking and critical analysis of findings.

Dunn, O. (2011) 'A unique child: home culture – worlds apart', *Nursery World*, 9 August.

Dunn summarises by introducing her article with 'To understand a child's home culture, early years educators need to look beyond the superficial, such as food and dress, to parents' ways of thinking, attitudes to behaviour and long-term aspirations for their children', with examples of a Chinese parent and philosophy influencing their expectations.

- Reflect on practice in the setting where you are employed or in placement on how culture is embedded in the daily routine.
- How would you ensure cultures of all children are given importance?

Sarathchandra, K.A.D.P (2008) 'Young children learning for sustainable development through traditional culture', in I. Pramling Samuelsson and Y. Kaga (eds), *Contribution of Early Childhood Education in a Sustainable Society*. Paris: UNESCO. Also available at: Http://unesdoc.unesco.org/images/0015/001593/159355e.pdf

This article highlights how children can be supported to develop their potential using local traditional knowledge, activities and resources to help in the holistic development, including physical, conceptual, social and spiritual/emotional development of children in early childhood.

- Discuss how you can use different traditional cultures of children to promote a child's holistic development.
- Reproduce the information relating to different areas of development using resources and activities from your own culture's perspective.

Ang Ling-Yin, L. (2007) 'Cultural diversity and the Curriculum Guidance for the Foundation Stage in England', *European Early Childhood Education Research Journal*, 15(2): 183–95.

This article focuses on how cultural diversity is promoted in early childhood education making references to curriculum guidance for

Continues

Continued

the foundation stage in England. The article uses discourse analysis as methodology.

- Summarise the key issues from this article.
- What are the challenges in promoting different cultures in an early childhood setting?
- How does it compare to the current context of EYFS?

Vandenbroeck, M., Roets, G. and Snoeck, A. (2009) 'Immigrant mothers crossing borders: nomadic identities and multiple belongings in early childhood education', *European Early Childhood Education Research Journal*, 17(2): 203–16.

This study draws on the narratives of three recently arrived immigrant mothers with young children, making use of childcare. The authors make links to different theories and analysis of the data. This article also provides an insight into use of narratives as a methodology.

- Explore repeating the study on a smaller scale.
- What is the relevance of the theories related to in this article to a British setting?

Gregory, E. and Ruby, M. (2011) 'The "insider/outsider" dilemma of ethnography: working with young children and their families in cross-cultural contexts', *Journal of Early Childhood Research*, 9(2): 162–74.

The authors make references to their dilemmas not explained by theories and their confusions and contradictions about different cultures. How to use ethnography as a research method.

- Discuss key issues of this article in groups.
- Reflect on the dilemmas referred to in the article.

Further reading

Baldock, P. (2010) *Understanding Cultural Diversity in the Early Years*. London: Sage.

Lane, J. (2008) *Young Children and Racial Justice*. London: National Children's Bureau.

Siraj-Blatchford, I. and Clarke, P. (2005) *Supporting Identity, Diversity and Language in the Early Years*. Buckingham: Open University Press.

Useful websites

Bernard Van Leer foundation, http://www.bernardvanleer.org/.

Early Years Foundation Stage, http://www.education.gov.uk/childrenandyoung-people/earlylearningandchildcare/delivery/education/a0068102/early-years-foundation-stage-eyfs.

Department of Education, http://www.education.gov.uk/.

Teacher training resource bank is now available on: http://webarchive.nation-alarchives.gov.uk/20101021152907/http://www.ttrb.ac.uk/.

http://www.foundationyears.org.uk/.

4

EAL and inclusion

Chapter overview

This chapter aims to explore issues around English as an additional language (EAL) in the early childhood context. These include the contexts in which children and their families will be bi- and/or multi-lingual. The theoretical background to the acquisition of language and the abilities of bilingual and multilingual children to communicate in appropriate languages with different people is highlighted. The advantages and disadvantages related to being bilingual or multilingual are discussed.

Are children disadvantaged or are they labelled as slow learners if they are not able to speak English? Do practitioners consider it an opportunity or a hassle to have a child who is able to speak languages other than English, or the majority language? How can a practitioner cope with children who are bilingual/multilingual? Are bilingual/multilingual children excluded from mainstream activities due to being unable to communicate in English with their peers and adults in the setting?

It has been reported that there are 6,000 languages spoken around the world (UNESCO, 2011). By the end of the twenty-first century, several languages, especially indigenous ones, may be at risk of being endangered as a result of colonial rule across the world. UNESCO'S director general warns:

The death of a language leads to the disappearance of many forms of intangible cultural heritage, especially the invaluable heritage of traditions and oral expressions of the community that spoke it – from poems and legends to proverbs and jokes. The loss of languages is also detrimental to humanity's grasp of biodiversity, as they transmit much knowledge about nature and the universe. (UNESCO, 2009)

In England, 16.8 per cent of children above compulsory school age belonged to families whose mother tongue was not English (DfE, 2011a). However, there are regional differences with a higher number of bilingual children in certain areas. For example, according to new research published in 2010 by the Institute of Education and CILT (the National Centre for Languages), 41 per cent of state school pupils are able to speak another language in addition to English. This report also mentions that 42 languages are spoken across London by more than 1,000 pupils and 12 languages are spoken by more than 10,000 pupils (Eversley et al., 2010).

Bilingualism is an asset, and the first language has a continuing and significant role in identity, learning and the acquisition of additional languages (DCSF, 2007). UNESCO has promoted the use of mother tongue to instruct children at early childhood and primary level since 1953 (Ball, 2010). Countries around the world are monolingual or multilingual. Some countries have one official language, however people speak more indigenous languages. Some are bilingual countries, such as Canada (French and English), or are multilingual, such as Mexico, which recognises 62 indigenous languages. The USA has different languages dominant apart from English in some states. For example, Louisiana has English and French; California, Texas and Florida have Spanish and English. A majority of Asian countries are bilingual and multilingual. For example India has 23 official languages, including English. Several European countries are bilingual or trilingual. For example, Belgium has three official languages (Dutch, French and German); Finland has two official languages, Finnish and Swedish. Luxembourg is a trilingual country with Luxembourgish, French and German. Yet, monolingualism is still the norm around the world, for example in countries such as France, Italy, Portugal and Germany. In England, English is the only language spoken predominantly and a tiny minority speak Cornish. Wales is a bilingual country with Welsh afforded an official status. The Welsh language is protected by the Welsh Language Act 1993 and the Government of Wales Act 1998. In Scotland, English is the dominant language although Gaelic is also spoken by a small minority. According to the Scottish government website, 1.15 per cent of the Scottish population speak Gaelic. However, the majority of countries, in spite of having one official language, are proficient in more than one language due to having borders with a neighbouring country speaking another language.

In addition to the languages spoken it is important to consider the number of deaf people and their families who are able to communicate in British sign language. Children and adults who are unable to communicate in the dominant language are at risk of being excluded and special efforts need to be introduced to promote inclusion. Children and their families are to be respected by recognising their linguistic needs to communicate, whether verbally or in any other form such as sign language.

What is bilingualism?

Young children from every corner of the world are learning languages that are different from the dominant language used in their own country, due to globalisation. Families are moving around for several reasons such as immigration, seeking asylum, better jobs or job transfers due to globalisation of companies. These children arrive at school with a precious resource – their mother tongue.

Typically, when children begin pre-school, they are expected to learn the language dominant in their area to be included. Most often, these children are educated exclusively in the dominant language, which will be a second language. A majority of early childhood settings do not consider it important to support development and competence in the minority language. A bilingual child may not possess proficiency at the same level in both languages. As a young child, proficiency in the mother tongue may be better than the second or third language (which may be the dominant language). The level of proficiency may shift from mother tongue to the dominant language with the child's transition from home to school.

When attending an early childhood setting, sometimes children are forced to switch abruptly from their mother tongue to the dominant language. As a result, children may lose their proficiency in their mother tongue. In addition, their self-confidence as learners and their interest in their environment may decline, leading to lack of motivation, school failure and early school leaving.

Contexts of inclusion and exclusion

English is a widely spoken and globalised language. This makes English a powerful language. Several countries where English is not the first language are introducing English at a young age, at pre-school, so that children gain a good level of proficiency. On the other hand, Clyne (1991) reported that children from migrant families have acquired limited and receptive understanding of their mother tongue. Early childhood education and schooling reproduced inequality and power relations between various cultural and language groups resulting in families preferring their children to learn English and not their mother tongue, in an attempt to be included successfully in the mainstream community.

Statistics

The contexts of inclusion and exclusion may vary from one setting to another. Children, often neglected or ignored, especially by peers, when they are unable to speak the local language, are struggling to communicate with their peers. If a practitioner is familiar with a European language spoken by the child and his or her family such as French, Spanish or German, then they may feel confident to communicate in either their mother tongue or perhaps in English if parents are comfortable. Attitudes of early childhood practitioners towards a particular minority language may influence a child's ability to maintain speaking their mother tongue, preventing them from shifting fully to the dominant language. This will allow all languages spoken in the community to be active and help prevent language death in society.

In the 1950s and 1960s children from working-class immigrant and indigenous communities were stereotyped as underachievers. This was referred to as the deficit model or cultural deprivation. However, a worldwide trend of children from immigrant Indian and Chinese families achieving well academically has been reported by current research and a government report (DCSF, 2008). On the other hand, this report also pointed to the fact that children from immigrant families were labelled as SEN due to poor assessment of their needs. Some of the findings included:

Young children who have EAL do less well, especially in tests of verbal skills, and children with EAL perform better in non-verbal tests. The gap reduces between the ages of 3 and 7 as children's fluency in English improves.

Ethnicity is associated with a few differences in early literacy and numeracy achievement up to age 5.

Most apparent differences between children from different ethnic groups are due to poverty and EAL.

Effective provision for pre-school education (EPPE), a longitudinal study conducted in England, reported that the home learning environment has a greater influence on a child's intellectual and social development than parental occupation, education or income (Sylva et al., 2009). What parents do is more important than who they are, and a home environment that is supportive of learning can counteract the effects of disadvantage in the early years.

Exclusion and inclusion

Child's perspective
- Why can't they understand me?
- They are all better than me.
- I think they do not like me.
- They will laugh if I speak in my language.
- I am scared, why do they shout at me?
- What have I done, I would like to play with all children.
- I want to talk with everybody. How can I? I don't know how to talk with these children.
- I am not intelligent.
- Why can't I play with these children?

Figure 4.1 Child's perspective of EAL

Parent's perspective – I do not know how to talk in English. I do not have any time to spend with the child or the practitioner to help them to understand the home language. I can't understand what they want, what the practitioner means. Can I ask this question again? What will others think? I do not want to create unnecessary problems. Is this a stupid question?

Practitioner's perspective – How do I help? What can I do? Who can help? What resources are available? How can I pass the message to parents? What other ways are there to communicate with this child and parents? Can I engage this parent in any activity to enable the child to develop positive self-esteem?

Importance of the mother tongue

The EYFS emphasises the role of the mother tongue in laying strong foundations in language development. It is crucial to encourage the use of the mother tongue in the home environment. Proficiency in home language will help maintain positive family connections. If a child speaks the majority language and loses their ability to speak their mother tongue, this might impact on their ability to have proper meaningful conversations with elderly family members who may not understand the child's accent. Parents who are unable to talk with their children in their mother tongue, may gradually lose their ability to influence their values and beliefs. The implication for the child and family of losing proficiency in the mother tongue is illustrated in the example below.

A young child from an immigrant family used to speak fluent Arabic. His parents encouraged him to speak English before he started nursery so that he could settle down comfortably in the new setting. The child settled down well after being welcomed by the practitioner and the peer group. The child was happy to be included by the setting and made several friends as he was able to express himself in English. His parents, who were both well educated, did not mind continuing to communicate in English.

When grandparents visited after three months, they realised that this child was struggling to express himself with them and later tried to detach himself from them. They found their grandchild's behaviour unusual and a bit distressing. Parents and grandparents discussed and reflected on their experiences from the past few weeks, and realised that the child was losing his proficiency in his mother tongue. They concluded that they needed to respond to the situation instantly.

The parents discussed this incident with the practitioner and the setting, and sought advice. As a practitioner, what steps would you take to revive this child's proficiency in his mother tongue sensitively? What measures would you take to make any subtle changes in the routine in the setting to encourage this child to use Arabic in the setting with pride? How would you engage parents and/or grandparents in the setting to help the setting raise their awareness of different cultures and languages?

Tickell (2011) recommends children are supported in their language development from an early age and also emphasises encouraging them to develop their mother tongue so that they are able to express themselves and be understood by their extended family members. She also suggests that EYFS framework should be made accessible to all parents by redrafting it in plain English and avoiding complicated words and jargon.

Advantages of being a bilingual:

1. The child will be praised by parents and their friends as well as practitioners for being a smart child, able to learn and use more than one language fluently. In countries where monolingualism is the norm, bilingual children will be appreciated for their multilinguistic abilities. This will result in improved self-esteem and confidence.

2. The child will be able to develop mature thinking at an early age.

This will enable the child to empathise with other bilingual children and take the initiative to support them.

3. Bilingual children typically develop certain types of cognitive flexibility and meta-linguistic awareness earlier and better than their monolingual peers.

4. Awareness of different languages will enrich the child's ability to relate to how different languages work. This will help them to learn new languages with relatively less effort and be able to learn new words easily. Research has reported better such abilities in bilingual children than in their monolingual peers.

5. Slightly older children sometimes act as interpreters for their parents and practitioners, and mentors or buddies for their peers (children), especially those who cannot speak English in the nursery.

How do children become bilinguals?

Children in several countries are growing up to learn more than one language. Many children may acquire two languages from birth and may start a formal setting as bilinguals. Bilingual children usually learn another language in informal settings such as within the home, where one or both parents can speak another language. In addition they may learn from friends while playing in the neighbourhood or from watching television, or from the nanny speaking in her native language.

Bilingual children develop empathy towards others who are unable to speak in the dominant language and are sensitive to other cultures and languages. They will feel sympathy for immigrants and empathy for their children, and are less likely to be prejudiced. Bilingualism will enable children to develop an understanding and awareness of more than one culture.

Theoretical base

Definition of language

Language has been defined as 'the formation and communication of information, thoughts and feelings in the form of words' (Gonzales-Mena, 1998: 324). 'Language is used to communicate and convey meaning from one person to another. It is used to talk to each other, write and email and text. Language has rules which involve word structure (morphology), grammar and sentence structure (syntax), word meaning (semantics) and social appropriateness (pragmatics)' (Gonzales-Mena, 1998: 324).

Siraj Blatchford and Clarke (2000: 20) explain language as involving:

> more than learning a linguistic code with which to label the world or to refer to abstract concepts, language also involves learning how to use the code in socially appropriate and effective ways. It is not just a question of learning the words and grammar of another language; you must also know how to use them in socially acceptable ways.

Terminology

The terminology around bilingualism is complex. The terms change in different contexts in regional, national and international contexts. Some of them include ESOL (English speakers of other languages), EMAS (ethnic minority achievement service) and ethnic minorities achievement teams (EMAs or EMATs) for every local authority. English as an additional language (EAL) is the expression used in the UK to refer to the teaching of English to speakers of other languages. Current statistics indicate that almost 10 per cent of pupils in maintained schools are learning English as a second, third or, indeed, fourth language, in addition to the language spoken in their families, and over 300 languages are spoken by pupils in UK schools.

The mother tongue may be the first language and also the language spoken at home and to which a child is exposed. However, home language may not be the mother tongue as parents may speak the dominant language, such as English.

Several countries start using the children's mother tongue in early childhood settings for easy transition. However, countries such as India introduce at least two or three languages in most of the government schools at primary school level – regional language and national language, as well as English as a global language. For example, a child starting school in Mumbai, capital of Maharashtra, would learn Marathi – the vernacular language spoken locally – in addition to Hindi (national language) and English.

Dimensions of bilingualism

Baker (2006) has analysed issues around bilingualism and multi-lingualism along the following dimensions: ability, use, balance of two or more languages, age of children, development of language, culture, contexts and elective bilingualism.

1. Ability – a child might develop varied abilities in different

languages. The skills relate to listening (understanding), speaking, reading and writing. The ability can be categorised as active and passive bilingualism. Active bilingualism relates to the ability to speak and write in both languages. Passive bilingualism is about an individual being in different stages of acquiring a second language; for example, to understand, to speak, to read and write.

2. Use of languages – the opportunities for an individual to use languages in different contexts such as at home, at school, in the street, on the telephone and on television, and for different purposes to communicate with family, friends, school – through the medium of teaching and learning and programmes watched on television, and childcare contexts – and languages spoken with the childminder, nanny or at breakfast or after school clubs.

3. Balance of two or more languages – the ability of an individual to have the competence to speak in different languages may not be the same. The ability to speak one language may be better than the others due to its dominant use in different contexts.

4. Age – when children learn two languages from birth it is called simultaneous or infantile bilingualism. For example, a baby will be exposed to two languages when a baby's parents speak different languages and speak to the baby in their mother tongue from birth. On the other hand, if a second language is learnt after three years it is termed consecutive or sequential bilingualism.

5. Development – an individual's ability and competence in different languages may vary at different stages. For example, one language may be well developed and the other may be in the early stages of speaking or understanding.

6. Culture – bilinguals will be bicultural or multicultural. It is difficult to have proficiency in more than one language. A person who is bicultural can still be monocultural. On the other hand, a person who is monolingual may be bicultural – an immigrant learning the local or indigenous language will relate to the process of acculturation. An individual's awareness of more than one culture and competence in more than one language and culture will encourage them to develop right attitudes towards both cultures, enabling them to behave in culturally appropriate ways and with the confidence to express themselves appropriately.

7. Contexts – some individuals may live in bilingual and multilingual societies that use more than one language. In other contexts individuals may choose to learn a second or third language by choice or may be demanded by the requirements of their

job and to work effectively, which is referred to as circumstantial bilingualism. For example, immigrants working in different countries in the European Union may have to learn the local language to operate in the immediate society. Sometimes, monolingual societies may promote the dominant language, resulting in the child's first language being replaced by the second language. This enables the individual (adult or child) to be better accepted by their peer group. This could include immigrants, diplomats, expatriates, and so on.

8. Elective bilingualism – some individuals might opt to become bilingual. They learn another language for personal or professional reasons. A mother who arrives in a new country with her children may be forced to learn the local language, for example by attending ESOL classes, to function effectively. It is highly unlikely for a mother to lose her first language. In other instances, individuals may have to learn a second language owing to the requirements of their circumstances. As a result of circumstantial bilingualism, an individual's status improves and they may move up the career ladder.

Balance theory

This theory refers to how two languages exist in balance in a child's head. Is one of the languages weighing more heavily at the expense of the first language? Another analogy representing a bilingual child is two language balloons in a child's head. For a monolingual, there is one balloon that is fully filled. On the other hand, a bilingual child has two half-filled balloons that might lead to confusion, frustration and failure. Cummins (1980) referred to this as the separate underlying proficiency model of bilingualism. This model represents two languages operating separately without transfer and with a limited amount of room for each of the languages.

However, research has also pointed out that the human brain is able to accommodate more than two languages. This theory contradicts the balloon or balance theory. In addition, language attributes are not separated, but transfer readily and are interactive. This exchange of information in different languages led to an alternative concept – the common underlying proficiency model of bilingualism (Cummins, 1980, 1981). This model is represented as two icebergs (languages) that on the surface are integrated into one iceberg. Although a child is able to function in two languages, he or she is readily able to transfer information from one language to another. Early concepts such as basic numbers learnt in the mother tongue can still be used at a later age in mathematical problem-solving at a higher level where the concepts are learnt in a different language, such as English or French.

Vygotsky's theory suggests that development occurs on the social level within a cultural context and language is a major channel used by adults to initiate children into developing a particular view of the world (Vygotsky, 1978). Vygotsky also considered acquisition of language as a major milestone of cognitive development in addition to facilitating thought and organising knowledge. The zone of proximal development (ZPD) represents how children can learn a first or second language with support from adults (parent/carer or practitioner).

Young children who are bilinguals are able to use both languages in the early childhood setting which is referred to as 'code switching' where children use words from other languages or switch languages in the middle of a conversation. Two types of language acquisition have been described – simultaneous and sequential or successive acquisition. Simultaneous acquisition occurs when children are learning both languages at the same time from an early age, for example when both parents speak different languages. Sequential or successive acquisition occurs when the first language is partially learnt. For example, after learning the mother tongue at home, a child may learn an additional language (for example, English or Spanish) in the early childhood setting or from the nanny. Sometimes, a child may be exposed to more than two languages in different contexts, for example, at home, in early childhood settings, from the nanny, peers or television programmes.

Types of bilinguals

The extent to which a person is bilingual can vary. Some people are equally proficient in two languages across a range of contexts and this is often referred to as 'balanced bilingualism'. More often, when people are bilingual, one of the languages is used more regularly and with greater proficiency. This may be referred to as 'dominant bilingualism'. There are also people who understand and use three or more languages, and may be referred to as 'multilingual'.

There are two main ways to acquire more than one language:

- simultaneous acquisition (when a child learns two languages at the same time), and

- sequential acquisition (when the second language is learnt after the first).

Simultaneous acquisition

There are three identified stages when languages are acquired simultaneously:

Stage 1 – the child mixes two languages into one system.

Stage 2 – the child starts to separate the words from each language and recognises to which person that language should be spoken.

Stage 3 – one language is used more than the other and that language becomes dominant, which is often the case.

In simultaneous acquisition, there are two common patterns of exposure to a second language:

• One person, one language (for example, where one parent or other family member speaks one language, and another parent or family member speaks a different language), or

• Both parents (and other family members) speak both languages. In general, the 'one person, one language' approach helps children to separate and learn both languages.

Sequential acquisition

There are also three identified stages which motivate and guide sequential language learners:

Stage 1 – the child listens to speakers of the second language and may be silent; the child may communicate non-verbally (for example, pointing); later, the child relies on whole memorised phrases.

Stage 2 – the child communicates with others in the second language; the child starts to create their own sentences; the child communicates as best they can.

Stage 3 – the child attempts to speak correctly using correct vocabulary.

Role of adults in language acquisition

Vygotsky (1978) and Bruner (1983) have emphasised the importance of social context in language development. Social experiences influence the children's thinking and interpretation of events. Vygotsky (1978) believes language acquisition is a major milestone facilitated by interactions with adults and children. Vygotsky's zone of proximal development has demonstrated that scaffolding can enable the child to learn languages. Parents and practitioners in an early childhood setting may use a range of strategies such as demonstrating and modelling, turn-taking, questioning and providing stimulation through different sources.

Parents make language choices in terms of conscious, subconscious and spontaneous decisions. Emotions affect language choices and strategies. Different languages are used by parents to convey the emotions of praise and discipline, love and instructions. Different languages are used by individuals to convey messages effectively.

For example, some children whose first language is not English may not be able to respond to the standard assessments in English owing to their poor English skills. New Zealand is admired for its bicultural and bilingual society. This is reflected in all its governmental communication being in two languages – English and Maori. In a lot of European countries more than one language is spoken. In the United Kingdom, there are children learning their mother tongue in Saturday schools which can be in a formal or informal setting; for example, Mandarin, Arabic, Punjabi, Telugu, Tamil and Bengali.

English is a widely spoken and globalised language. Widespread use of the English language resulted in inequality and hierarchical power relations between various cultural and language groups. Families preferred their children to learn English and not their mother tongue in an attempt to be included successfully in the mainstream community. So, several countries where English is not the first language are introducing English at a young age at pre-school level so that children will achieve a good level of proficiency. As a result, the abilities of children from migrant families to understand and speak their mother tongue will be restricted. Therefore, early childhood settings must encourage the use of the children's home languages and not replace them with English. For bilingual children and adults, the linguistic habits generated in speaking English and the home language or dialect will undergo various adaptations and transformations. When children from ethnic minority families start at a formal early childhood setting in an English-speaking country, such as England, the USA or Australia, they face strong pressure from peers and adults to assimilate into the local culture and language. The children attempt to learn to speak English to be accepted by other children and adults (early childhood practitioners). As their proficiency in English improves, they will use their mother tongue less, leading to a loss of fluency or vocabulary, or even forgetting their home language entirely.

The consequences of poor proficiency in their home language will result in poor self-esteem, and undervaluing their language and culture. This will gradually cause breaks in family relationships, especially with older members (grandparents), owing to children's inability to communicate in their home language. Further, older family members will struggle to pass on the family values, morals and values, traditions, beliefs and family wisdom to the child owing to the lack of ability to communicate.

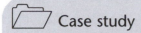 Case study

A 2-year-old child from a Polish family starts nursery. This child is able to speak Polish. When this child started nursery, he had problems settling down as staff in the nursery could not understand Polish. As the parents could speak some English, the nursery manager suggested to the parents that they speak to the child only in English so that the child can feel comfortable and settle in the nursery. Parents of this child expressed to the practitioner that they did not feel comfortable speaking in English with their child.

- As a practitioner, how would you respond to this situation?
- What are the advantages and disadvantages of the family encouraging the child to speak in English in all contexts?
- What strategies can you use to encourage the child to settle down comfortably in the setting?
- How will you encourage the child to learn English without losing the child's first language?
- What are the ways in which you will communicate with the child effectively?

Evidence from several studies indicates that children are more likely to use, process and comprehend like native speakers when they learn a second language at a young age. This is due to neuronal structures in the brain being optimally responsive to the stimulation. This is called the 'critical period' for learning languages. When parents of the child speak in different languages, the child may be able to speak both the languages. In some situations, if the child is exposed to more than two languages, the child will be able speak all the languages that he/she is exposed to. Further, the child will be able to differentiate and switch languages appropriately with the individuals. For example, mother may speak French, father may speak Arabic, nanny may speak Russian and English may be spoken in the childcare settings.

Research suggests that children as young as 2 years are able to speak different languages and are able to switch between languages appropriately with the individuals. For example, an Indian American family with a 2-year-old child encouraged their child to speak different languages. He spoke with mum in Telugu (a language spoken in South India), with dad in Gujarati (a language spoken in North India), in the nursery in English and with nanny in Russian.

Legislation

Legislation and policy at global, national and setting levels influence practice. At the global level the UNCRC has strongly recommended all countries to empower children to access their rights through the 52 articles. This has been ratified by all countries except Somalia and the USA. Article 30 of the UNCRC states that you have a right to learn and use the language and customs of your family whether or not these are shared by the majority of the people in the country where you live.

At the national level, Section 312 of the Education Act 1996 stipulates:

> A child must not be regarded as having a learning difficulty solely because the language or form of language of the home is different from the language in which he or she is or will be taught. Thus children learning EAL may have SEN, but that must not be assumed if the only reason for their learning difficulties is that they do not initially speak the language of the school. (DfEE, 1996)

The Equality Act 2010 (DfE, 2010b) has replaced all existing equality legislation related to discrimination against children and adults – parents and practitioners. This Act recommends that all early childhood settings ensure they regularly review practices, policies and procedures. This is to ensure that people with a 'protected characteristic' should not be discriminated against. The setting must make sure that it cannot unlawfully discriminate against pupils based on their sex, race, disability, religion or belief or sexual orientation.

Examples of good practice

The population is becoming linguistically diverse owing to globalisation, so it is important to ensure the profile of early childhood practitioners, bilingual teachers and other professionals in early years and childcare reflects the diversity of children and families. If practitioners are bilingual, it will enable them to bring in their own personal and professional experience to support children and their families.

Local authorities provide a range of professionals and services such as bilingual practitioners, community officers or assistants or teams belonging to ethnic minority achievement services, or inclusion teams within Children's Services, early years or school improvement teams to help bilingual children.

Bilingual assistants in England were employed through Section 11 of the Local Government Act 1966, which made funding available to local authorities to support children from countries in the new Commonwealth. This was extended to cover all ethnic minority pupils through a Private Members Bill in 1993.

Activity

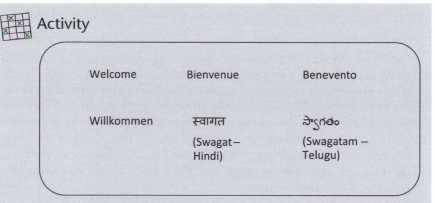

Figure 4.2 **Welcome poster**

The poster in Figure 4.2 contains a welcome message in different languages. As a practitioner, this poster can be used with children for discussion and analysis. Discussion could be around the number of languages spoken in the world, how many languages the children can speak and how many languages children are aware of and where these languages are spoken. Children could relate to the structure of letters in different languages. Using the linguistic skills of children in the setting, develop another unique poster based on phrases such as welcome, hello and thanks. Practitioners can encourage parents of bilingual children in the setting to make a list of common words in their languages.

There are several issues affecting a bilingual child in an early childhood setting. The child may not understand the language and the cultural contexts of the practitioner and the setting. The communication is not only verbal but also includes influence of culture on non-verbal communication. It is important to see how multicultural resources are used in a setting. For example, if a setting has a bilingual story book a practitioner may display the book to show that they do have multicultural resources that make their setting an inclusive setting. Another setting may encourage the parent of a bilingual child to borrow the bilingual book to read the story the night before so that the child can enjoy the story better on the following day along with the peer group.

The attitude of the practitioner is very important. If a practitioner questions the point of having a bilingual book in the setting as the children cannot read yet, it is a matter of how creative they can be in using the books in the setting. Similarly what is the point of having baby books?

Ensure children are provided space and time, patience and support, appropriate provision and recognition of their skills in their home language. This will give them confidence to achieve in English or the majority language. Children are natural linguists, who will be confident bilinguals enabling them to claim cognitive and social benefits.

Children are likely to exclude when a child speaks a language other than

Continues

Continued

English or the majority language, and if they are not familiar with the home language and culture of the child and his or her family. As a result of being excluded and being exposed to a new culture and language in the new environment with different expectations, the child may feel anxious and insecure in the new setting. Some of the settings make an extra effort to ensure the transition is smooth and all new children are comfortable in the new setting by collaborating and discussing with the parents to become familiar with some basic words in the child's home language and with their culture.

Organise events to promote bilingualism/multilingualism in the early childhood setting. Create a multilingual classroom. Encourage children to answer the register in different languages. Allow children to choose languages in which they might like to answer the register. Use bilingual sources – books and stories from different parts of the world. Help children to create stories in their own languages. Encourage children to talk in their home language whenever possible, even if it is only few words, and recognise this as a strength in contrast to a weakness of not being able to speak English or other native language. Use a welcome poster actively by discussing different languages spoken around the world. How many are the children aware of and where are they spoken?

Recruit bilingual practitioners to work with bilingual children as teaching assistants, school advisers, and to speak with families of EAL children. Invite parents and grandparents of children into the setting to interact with children to promote their awareness, knowledge and understanding of different languages. It is not uncommon to find community members, especially parents and grandparents, playing substantial roles in early childhood programmes, both to assist with language translation and to enhance the local cultural relevance of songs, games, stories and other curriculum content for young children and families. Irrespective of the recruitment of staff and/or children from ethnic minority families who do not speak the majority language, practitioners can encourage children to use a different language to register their attendance in the setting. Children may be asked to find out how a common word in English may be translated into different languages. An early childhood setting should adopt a positive attitude to its children's bilingualism and, whenever possible, should help maintain and deepen their knowledge of their mother tongue.

Wales is strongly involved in reviving the Welsh language, which was almost on the brink of extinction due to previous governments promoting the use of English. The Mudiad Ysgolion Meithrin – the Association of Welsh-medium playgroups (www.mym.co.uk), are prioritising early bilingualism by including resources and activities in Welsh in their programmes.

Debates and controversies

How can teachers be recruited and trained to deliver mother-tongue-based bilingual/multilingual programmes suitable for young children? Practitioners must be found with appropriate knowledge and skill to deliver appropriately to meet the needs of children and their families speaking different languages.

Is it better for a child to be exposed to one language rather than two languages? Bilingual children get included by staff and children in the early childhood settings if they are fluent in the majority language. Bilingual children can be at a disadvantage compared to monolingual children.

Do children have to learn the majority language at the cost of their mother tongue? Delays in speech and language development are caused by learning a second language. It is easier to learn a second language if you stop using your first or home language and concentrate on the new language. Should parents stop using the first or home language when the child begins speaking a second language, such as English?

Implications for practice

Encourage family members to work with early childhood practitioners on creating books in the local language. Use a range of ways (inviting them into the setting to tell the stories, use a camcorder, or use Skype to talk to children) to capture stories and music that the community values and wants to pass on to their children, as well as pictures of artefacts and typical home environments, common objects and local scenery.

Promote policies that place parents (and other family members) as 'first educators'. Encourage family members of EAL children to engage in all stages of programme planning, implementation and evaluation.

Consider the ability of a child to speak more than one language as an asset. Empower children speaking different languages by rewarding them.

Set up a peer support programme – encourage children to support each other, building on their strengths and overlooking weaknesses. Enlist the support of all staff members in producing bilingual or multilingual resources to raise awareness.

UNESCO affirms the critical role of parents as children's first language teachers. Raise awareness of parents' need for information about dual and plural language acquisition, and encourage parents to give priority to their children's acquisition of their mother tongue.

Use a range of resources to celebrate the linguistic diversity of the setting through use of Persona Dolls, music (live or recorded), and posters with simple words.

Share good practice with other early childhood practitioners by inviting them to the setting, or present your experiences in seminars, workshops or conferences in local, national or international conferences.

Raise the status of the setting by advertising the inclusivity of the setting by emphasising the number of bilingual children, and share good practice on support provided to these children.

Celebrate international mother language day on 21 February.

 Research issues

This section refers to research published on some significant EAL issues. Some of the issues that have been researched on aspects of EAL and inclusion include:

- The impact of bilingualism on children's language and cognitive development.
- Good practice around the ways in which bilingual children are supported.
- Practitioners' attitudes towards bilingualism.
- Strategies and resources to support bilingual children.
- Advantages and disadvantages of being a bilingual child.
- Parents' attitude to their child learning a second language.

The abstract for each research document is followed by questions that will stimulate thinking and critical analysis of findings.

Karmiloff, K. and Karmiloff-Smith, A. (2011) 'Native tongues', *Nursery World*, 111(4260): 14–16.

Two practitioners describe their experiences of providing opportunities to one of their first bilingual children and how they involved the child's parents in the nursery activities.

- What are the attitudes of practitioners towards bilingual children in different early childhood settings?

- What are the strategies used to involve bilingual parents in their children's learning?

Lao, C. (2004) 'Parents' attitudes towards Chinese English bilingual education and Chinese language use', *Bilingual Research Journal*, 28: 99–134.

Lao's study examines the strategies used in enabling English-Chinese bilingual pre-schoolers to develop their mother tongue. The perceptions of parents of bilingual education and their expectations about their children's future are explored. A range of advantages of being a bilingual child are indicated. This article points out the variation in the proficiency of the child's abilities in the Chinese language.

- Use a different research method to obtain information from parents about bilingualism.
- How can this study be repeated in a different setting?
- Compare and contrast the results obtained with the findings of Lao.

Grieve, A.M. and Haining, I. (2011) 'Inclusive practice? Supporting isolated bilingual learners in a mainstream school', *International Journal of Inclusive Education*, 15(7): 763–74.

This study explores the relationship between bilingualism and inclusion, examining official attitudes to bilingualism and the discrepancies realised between policy and practice relating to bilingual support to children.

- Discuss the findings of this research in small groups.
- Which strategies can be used to ensure the bilingual assistants in a mainstream school are supported?

Further reading

Baker, C. (1996) *Foundations of Bilingual Education and Bilingualism*. 2nd edn. Clevendon: Multilingual Matters.

Brooker, L. (2005) 'Learning to be a child: cultural diversity and early years ideology', in N. Yelland (ed.), *Critical Issues in Early Childhood Education*. Maidenhead: Open University Press.

Coghlan, M., Bergeron, C., White, K., Sharp, C., Morris, M. and Rutt, S. (2009) *Narrowing the Gap in Outcomes for Young Children Through Effective Practices in the Early Years*. London: Centre for Excellence and Outcomes in Children and Young People's Services (C4EO). Available at http://www.c4eo.org.uk/themes/earlyyears/ntg/files/c4eo_narrowing_the_gap_kr_1.pdf.

Karmiloff, K. and Karmiloff-Smith, A. (2011) 'Native tongues', *Nursery World*, 111(4260): 14–16.

Siraj-Blatchford, I. and Clarke, P. (2000) *Supporting Identity, Diversity and Language in the Early Years*. Buckingham: Open University Press.

Useful websites

National Association for language development in the curriculum, http://www.naldic.org.uk/.
National Centre for Languages, http://www.cilt.org.uk.
Languages without limits, http://www.languageswithoutlimits.co.uk/eal.html.
Multilingual family, http://www.multilingualfamily.org.uk.
Department for Education, http://www.education.gov.uk/.

5

Gypsy, Roma and Traveller (GRT) families and inclusion

Chapter overview

This chapter explores several key issues around Gypsy, Roma and Travellers (GRT) families. A variety of issues, such as attitudes of practitioners influenced by prejudices, poor knowledge and understanding, and lack of information about the services provided due to their nomadic lifestyle, influenced exclusion of children and their families. On the other hand, there are some GRT families who are not keen to send their children to early childhood settings or schools due to their own negative experiences. So, children from GRT families are included or excluded from mainstream early childhood settings by choice and/or they are excluded by the communities around them.

One of the main characteristics of GRT families is their mobility. Moving can be so frequent that children who travel with their family usually attend a new school every four or five days. Owing to restricted exposure to children from GRT families, practitioners tend to expand their preconceived stereotypes.

It has been widely recognised that GRT families are the most discriminated against and it has been referred to by Philips as a 'respectable form of racism' (2004). Some people blatantly voice their prejudices about GRT families. It is one of the groups in the community that has repeatedly been portrayed negatively in the media.

It is crucial for children in mainstream communities to have opportunities to develop a positive experience of GRT families from a young age, which will encourage them to accept and respect differences. In order to provide positive experiences to young children, it is important for early childhood practitioners and school teachers to confront their prejudices and redefine their perceptions, to develop a positive attitude towards GRT families.

Terminology

Some of the terms commonly used are nomads, itinerants and Travellers; they are groups of people who shift from one place to another regularly, rather than stay permanently in one place. There are an estimated 30–40 million nomads in the world. Many communities have traditionally been nomadic. However, several GRT families made a shift in their lifestyle resulting in settling down in a house. The term nomads commonly refers to those people who are constantly on the move. This form of livelihood is still seen in places such as Lapland, Mongolia, Kenya and many other countries. In Europe, people who do not have a stable home and are on the lookout for food and work are called Travellers.

The term Traveller covers a number of different groups with different histories and cultures. Gypsy, Roma and Traveller include English and Welsh Gypsies, Roma, Irish Travellers, Scottish and Welsh Travellers, Fairground Travellers, Showmen, Circus Travellers, Housed Travellers, New Travellers and Bargee Travellers.

English and Welsh Gypsies, Roma/Romany Gypsies are the largest group of Travellers in the UK. They originated in India and migrated in the Middle Ages, arriving in Britain in the fifteenth century; most have come from Eastern Europe and are living in houses.

One of the oldest groups is Irish Travellers, who are descended from established traders. Groups of Scottish Travellers developed, between 1500 and 1800, from travelling Scottish craft workers, who married into immigrant Romany groups from France and Spain. Welsh Travellers entered Wales around 1700 and spoke Romani. The majority of Welsh Travellers are now living in houses.

The term New Traveller refers to those groups of people from settled communities who adopted a travelling way of life. Bargee Travellers are those who live and work on barges. The population of this group is diminishing due to reduced use of canals as a means of transport.

All the groups above have been categorised as a single group because of their nomadic lifestyle, but they differ in the languages they speak, their traditions, ethnicity and lifestyles. For example, many Gypsies speak the inherited language of Romanes, while Irish Travellers may speak Cant or Gamon.

They may prefer to be referred to as Gypsies or Roma or Traveller families. Some of the terminology referring to Travellers families has often been used in a derogatory way. For example, the terms gyppo, pikey and tinker are considered to be highly insulting to many people and are considered to be racist. The term 'Gypsy' has been used as a term of abuse. So, some families dislike the term 'Gypsy'; for example, Irish Travellers often do not like to be called Gypsies and prefer to be called Travellers or Romanies or Roma. However, some choose to be called Gypsies, while others use the terms New Age Traveller, New Traveller or just Traveller. It is important to refer to Traveller with a capital T, to avoid being confused with other travellers who are not part of this group. People refer to Gypsy and Romany synonymously and interchangeably. It is advisable for early childhood practitioners and school teachers to clarify with individual families their preferred terminology to address them. The terms Gypsy and Travellers must be written with a capital first letter as a mark of respect to their group identity. Gypsy, Roma and Traveller is the accepted form of terminology.

The terms referring to the services provided to children and their families differ from one authority to another. The term Traveller Education Support Service (TESS) is used in some authorities. Some local authorities use Traveller Education Service (TES) and others use variations of Ethnic Minority and Traveller Achievement Service (EMTAS). Some LEAs have set up the Traveller Achievement Service (TAS) to meet the education needs of all Traveller children who reside or are travelling in their area.

Definition

The Gypsy/Traveller population of the United Kingdom now includes several distinct groups: Scottish Travellers, English Gypsies, Irish Travellers and Welsh Gypsies. Britain has also seen a rise in a non-traditional group of travelling folks, known as New Age Travellers. The Gypsies and Traveller population has been recognised as a racial group since 1988. The term 'Travellers' covers a wide range of groups, each with their own culture, ethnic background and patterns of mobility.

Irish Travellers share a common heritage in general terms and are highly mobile, travelling mainly between urban areas. They continue to experience significant levels of rejection and discrimination for being Irish, as well as for being Travellers. It has been 200 years since Irish Travellers first came to Britain. English Law has recognised Irish Travellers as an ethnic group since 1999 and they are recognised as an ethnic minority group under the Race Relations Act 1976. It is over 500 years since Romany Gypsies arrived in Britain. They are the largest ethnic minority in Europe, comprising 8 to 10 million people, and are also one of the most disadvantaged. The Roma populations across European countries descend from India, and as such share a heritage with some members of travelling communities in the UK.

Circus and fairground families prefer to be called 'Showmen', and together with Bargees, have their own traditional occupations. Circus and fairground families do not define themselves as Gypsies and their reasons for travelling are economic rather than cultural. At the start of the nineteenth century many cities had a permanent circus as well as travelling shows and circuses. Families learn their skills at a young age and these skills are handed down from generation to generation.

New Travellers emerged in the 1980s and 1990s, choosing to opt out of a mainstream lifestyle and to travel for a variety of reasons. New Travellers tend to have a positive attitude towards education, and while some children attend local schools for a short period of time, many families may still prefer to educate their children at home.

Some facts about GRT families

There are several myths about GRT children and families.

Some of the commonly held misconceptions about travellers' families include:

1. All Gypsies and Travellers are nomadic.

2. Travellers are thieves and criminals and dirty.

3. Gypsies and Travellers cannot read or write.

Practitioners may be influenced by these myths and prejudiced in their demeanour, and with low expectations of GRT children. In contrast to the stereotype, about half of the GRT population in UK live in houses, some on private or local authority sites. However, some are still nomadic.

Children are of prime importance to GRT families, and their care and welfare are central to Gypsy society. Education is important in the primary phase because Gypsy families want their children to have basic literacy skills. However, the nomadic lifestyle, and the expectation that children support the family's work, often force children to be absent from school.

Education is valued in its widest sense, and school is not the only place in which to receive education. Children are encouraged to take responsibility with helping with work and domestic chores, in addition to learning specific skills from their parents. Children may underachieve due to erratic attendance at school, and not necessarily due to SEN.

GRT families follow strict codes of cleanliness. Their children are highly valued, and their views listened to and respected.

Families are proud of their culture, but often prefer not to acknowledge it publicly owing to discrimination and racism. Parents' poor literacy skills may restrict them from accessing written communication from school and/or supporting their children with literacy activities.

Statistics

Statistics indicate discrepancies in establishing the exact number of Gypsy and Travellers in the country (DfES, 2003). This discrepancy is a result of several factors, such as some families may choose not to reveal their identity for fear of being prosecuted or discriminated against. On the other hand, they may have decided not to belong to the category of Gypsy, Roma and Traveller families due to a change in their lifestyle and are no longer travelling. Further, due to the nature of their travelling lifestyle, it is difficult to track their figures. The census in 2011 has added a new category in England and Wales that will allow people to indicate their ethnic identity as a Gypsy or Travellers. This might help to ascertain the number of people belonging to GRT families and enable the government to provide appropriate services to meet their diverse needs. This is an interesting but difficult conundrum that will unravel when the 2011 census statistics are revealed. Would adding a new category encourage the families to feel confident to identify themselves or will the fear of discrimination outweigh their decision?

There are approximately 300,000 Gypsy/Travellers in Britain today (DfES, 2003). This figure differs considerably from official government statistics (based upon the bi-annual Caravan Count). This discrepancy is a result of these families choosing whether or not to identify themselves as belonging to GRT. A majority of sources estimate the population to be between 180,000 and 300,000 (many are believed to be living in houses).

Government initiatives

There are several initiatives that have been established to help and support children and families from GRT communities. However, some of these initiatives are available to GRT families only in specific local authorities.

Every Gypsy, Roma and Traveller Child a Talker (E-GRT-CAT) has been developed in partnership with Education Leeds Gypsy Roma and Traveller Achievement Service, Leeds Speech and Language Therapy Service and Leeds City Council Early Years Service. It is based on the National Strategies project – the Every Child a Talker (ECAT) programme. The programme will strengthen children's early language development. This initiative can ensure that early childhood practitioners provide a learning environment in which GRT children and their families feel welcomed, respected and valued. Early childhood practitioners are supported to listen to children and their families in addition to developing a rich learning environment with relevant resources that reflects GRT culture as well as creative and challenging learning opportunities.

Gypsy Roma and Traveller History Month was launched in 2008 by the Department for Children, Schools and Families (DCSF) to explore GRT history and culture. As part of this initiative, schools, councils and other public bodies work together to challenge the myths, tackle stereotypes and celebrate the achievements of GRT children and their families. Schools encourage children to create a story, poem, painting or photographs portraying GRT culture or their history. This takes place in June every year.

In addition, there are several initiatives at local level funded by local authorities or voluntary organisations that are supporting GRT families to access services to meet their needs in the local areas. Friends, Families and Travellers is a national charity that provides advice and outreach services to all Gypsies and Travellers, regardless of ethnicity, culture or background. The charity facilitates and mentors local self-support groups to empower individuals, families and communities and share good practice about working with GRT families. It also provides training to voluntary and statutory organisations to provide appropriate and culturally sensitive services to Gypsies and Travellers.

Contexts of inclusion and exclusion

The services provided to GRT families and their children vary depending on the needs of the communities. Outreach services enable the GRT families to access services that have been adapted to meet their individual needs. Outreach services also facilitate GRT families to get to know the majority communities. The outreach services can be provided in family homes, site cabins, mobile library, or common grounds close to the caravan sites.

There are different examples of good practice in relation to provision for GRT children and families in England. Some examples include Norfolk TES working in partnership with a local children's centre. The services include a toy library and play sessions to support children and their families with transition into settings. Another service is a play bus provided in partnership between a local children's centre, voluntary organisation and local council. Some councils such as Nottinghamshire and Derbyshire use government programmes such as children's centres and Sure Start programmes in using play bag and learning bus as well as resources reflecting diverse cultures. A children's centre in Ellesmere Port in the north-west of England encourages mothers to attend adult learning classes while providing childcare for their children at the same premises. This indicates that the diversity of services provided to GRT families and children may be tailored around the needs of the community. However, the travel education service teams did not always include early years workers. The teams that included early years workers mostly work part-time. Further, a huge variation was found in their experience and qualifications.

Outreach play service provides an opportunity to build an equal and respectful relationship with children and their parents. Some of the resources, for example, animal toys, hobbyhorses and mobile home play trailers, can be borrowed by the family for a limited time, allowing the children to be creative and not influenced by practitioners and their beliefs.

Challenges

Practitioners may be working with a group of children belonging to a wide age range, owing to families with a large number of children. Working in a caravan site can be challenging as practitioners may not be aware of the values and beliefs of GRT families and communities. Practitioners must be sensitive to those values and traditions.

Practitioners may plan and prepare play experiences that are not convenient in the caravan – for example, messy or noisy activities. However, open discussion with parents can be useful to negotiate and provide solutions.

The location of caravans may limit the types of activities and play experiences presented to children It may be difficult to organise messy and water-based activities as these families have a strict code of cleanliness and limited space in their caravans. Risk assessments may have to be carried out and parents consulted to find a safe out-door play area for sessions.

Barriers to inclusion

Young children belonging to GRT families are at risk of underachievement (DfES, 2003a). So, DfES suggest 'the most effective way to promote the achievement of Gypsy Traveller Children is to ensure they are able to gain early access to education during the Foundation Stage' (DfES, 2005: 2). However, early childhood settings and schools cited several reasons provided by GRT families for not accessing early childhood provision (D'Arcy, 2010). Some of the reasons include:

- Owing to constant movement from one place to another, GRT families may not be aware of any early childhood provision in the area. In addition, the settings may not be able to accommodate the child in the middle of the term.

- Some parents may be unable to access childcare services due to unplanned movements, or evictions from their campsite.

- There are some parents who believe mothers are responsible for taking care of young children and do not consider it appropriate to access childcare from a formal setting.

- Some parents who had a negative experience of attending schools may prefer their children not to go through the same experience.

Families accessing any services, including education, and early child-hood practitioners working with Gypsy, Roma and Traveller families often mention similar reasons for not accessing available services, such as:

- Parents have limited information about services available in the local authority.

- Many families experience isolation due to the location of their caravans away from the mainstream community. Also, families are often visiting, living or residing on sites that are situated on the periphery of communities.

- Unpredicted travel patterns, lack of permanent accommodation, or regular evictions make it unrealistic to access services.

- Priorities of families may focus on accessing basic services. Information about early childhood settings may not be an immediate priority as childcare may be the responsibility of mothers and other female members of the family.

- Highly mobile families, that is, those travelling or residing on unauthorised sites, are unlikely to have official addresses. This can be a barrier to accessing funded early education places whose systems rely on permanent addresses as a point of contact for the purpose of the child's safety.

- Dependency and lack of transport will restrict mothers from being able to transport their children to the early childhood setting. This will isolate families further from accessing services.

- GRT parents may not have experienced early years services themselves and may not be familiar with the systems.

- There may be limited places available in local settings. GRT families may arrive in an area when the early childhood settings may not be able to provide a place for the child.

- Parents of children from GRT families have concerns about the safety of their young children and the possibility being a victim of prejudice, racism and bullying. They may be concerned about the attitudes of other parents, supervisors and professionals, and the particular vulnerability of their child, being of such a young age.

Language matters

Many GRT children and their families speak English. Some children belonging to Roma families may speak East European languages, such as Polish or Slovak. English and Irish Gypsy and Traveller families may speak Romani (originally from Sanskrit) or Gaelic and their home languages may not be English. Owing to children's lack of speech and language skills, some have been wrongly diagnosed as having SEN. In addition they may be excluded from mainstream activities, owing to their poor language skills, by peers and practitioners.

Children from GRT families and achievement

The Plowden Report (1967) was one of the first documents to describe GRT families as the most deprived group in the country, estimating that only 10 per cent of GRT children accessed education. This was raised again in a discussion paper 'The education of travellers' children' (HMI, 1983). The Swann Report (1983) reiterated underachievement of children from Traveller families and indicated that Gypsies in school were discriminated against and stereotyped more than any other ethnic minority group. The Swann Report identified Gypsy and Traveller pupils as being strongly affected by many factors influencing the education of children from other minority ethnic groups. Almost 50 per cent of Gypsy or Roma Children and 52 per cent of Traveller children of Irish heritage are in the bottom 20 per cent of the Early Years Foundation Stage Profile in all 13 scales (DCSF, 2009a).

The introduction of a centralised funding stream enabled local educational authorities to bid for a grant that enables them to provide support to all children. This has led to the establishment of a Traveller Education Support Service (TESS) responsible for the education of children from GRT families. These children are supported by peripatetic teachers, classroom assistants and welfare officers.

Gypsy and Traveller children are four times more likely to be excluded for their unacceptable behaviour than are their peers. There is a general concern about the over-representation of ethnic minority pupils among those identified as having special educational needs (SEN). Irish Traveller pupils are 2.7 times more likely than other white British pupils to have SEN, and Gypsy/Roma pupils are 2.6 times more likely to have SEN. Lindsay et al. (2006) comment that these high levels appear to have a number of contributory factors, including negative teacher attitudes, racism and bullying, and a curriculum that does not take sufficient account of Traveller cultures and mobility.

Children from Travellers' families have been wrongly labelled as SEN – is it stereotyping of a Traveller or SEN which is responsible for underachievement? Teaching and learning styles are inappropriate to the needs of these children. Danaher et al. (2007: 31) quoted a response from a participant in their study:

> With reading, we always start with making our own books and things like that with the kids' own experiences. But the schools, they seem to see them … as somebody who can't do it and therefore you start at the beginning like a reception child. They don't see it as somebody who has a lot of experiences already and abilities, just not this one … they have real problems. They have a system set out of how children are supposed to learn and the order they are supposed to do it, and they want to follow it. They follow it slowly, even though the kid might be like a sponge.

A DfES (2005) research paper, using data from 2002/03, reported that Irish Travellers were the group most likely to be permanently excluded, with 0.51 per cent of Irish Traveller pupils permanently excluded. This represented nearly four times the overall exclusion rate of 0.13 per cent of all pupils. Gypsy/Roma pupils were the third mostly likely group to be excluded.

A range of factors, apart from mobility (chosen or enforced), has been explored in relation to the low levels of GRT educational participation, attendance and achievement. Racist harassment and bullying are the most prominent themes in all the studies. Jordan (2001) and Lloyd and Stead (2001) reported frequent name-calling experienced by Scottish Gypsy/Traveller and show children. It has been constantly reported that children from GRT tend to be blamed for retaliation while the original provocation is ignored. Many Gypsy and Traveller parents do not consider schools to be safe for their children owing to their experience of racism and name-calling, leading to self-exclusion. While some schools have good anti-racist policies and anti-bullying strategies, others may not be able to implement them effectively. As a result, neither children nor parents will have the confidence to report incidents of being bullied or called names.

Jordan (2001) comments that teachers tend to focus on social issues in relation to GRT children instead of prioritising academic achievement as they do for other children. The teachers operate from a cultural deficit model that problematises GRT cultures.

Many studies refer to the importance of the physical environment and curriculum reflecting positive images of Gypsy and Traveller cultures. The TESS has played a major role in creating positive attitudes by raising awareness among school and early childhood settings and communities.

Constant unplanned mobility, placement of the trailer sites, poor public transport and cultural barriers might prevent GRT families from accessing early years provision such as playgroups and nurseries. Children from GRT families refuse to attend school due to their negative experiences. Families' strong desire to protect their children from getting bullied may force families to not allow their children to attend any provision that is not welcoming and supportive. Further, head teachers are reluctant to offer a place to these children because of their poor attendance and weak performance generally that may impact on the school's place in league tables.

Many Travellers' children have been diagnosed as SEN as a result of their poor academic abilities. It has been noted that there is little consideration given to limited learning opportunities. Respect for Travellers can be manifested by making reference to their lifestyle in a positive manner.

Theoretical base

It is essential for practitioners and organisations to develop an awareness of different cultures so that they can tailor the services according to the needs of the communities. It is important for early childhood settings as well as schools to be aware of GRT families' needs and problems to be able to develop trust and to access the childcare provided for them. It has been recognised that, rather than being aware of different cultures at superficial level, cultural competence will enhance the ability and capacity of an individual or an organisation to provide good quality services to children and families from diverse cultures. Cultural competency will guarantee good quality services due to the commitment of the practitioner. This will eliminate conflicts between practitioners and communities which arise as a result of having inappropriate services imposed on them which are laden with cultural bias.

Papadopoulos, Tilki and Taylor proposed a model for developing cultural competence to help nursing practitioners to provide care services to patients across diverse cultures. This model has been adopted by Irish Community Care, Merseyside, to enable them to provide relevant services to GRT families and ensure their services meet the needs of the community. Figure 5.1, on page 107, taken from Papadopoulos et al. (2006), illustrates the model for developing cultural competence.

The model consists of four stages. Cultural awareness is the first stage, in which a practitioner or a teacher may reflect on their personal value base and beliefs. An awareness of own prejudices and stereotypes against certain groups in one's community will enable an early childhood practitioner to be ready to change and 'unlearn' their prejudiced attitudes.

Cultural knowledge is the second stage. In this stage, a practitioner can endeavour to raise their awareness by meeting these families with an open mind, thereby improving their knowledge and understanding as well as raising their awareness of the problems these families face.

The third stage is cultural sensitivity, that is, how early childhood practitioners perceive children and their families from GRT communities. Practitioners should empower families by providing appropriate information. Families might not want to share information about their children or their families unless they develop trust in the outsider. This is possible if they feel respected and accepted in the attitudes and language used.

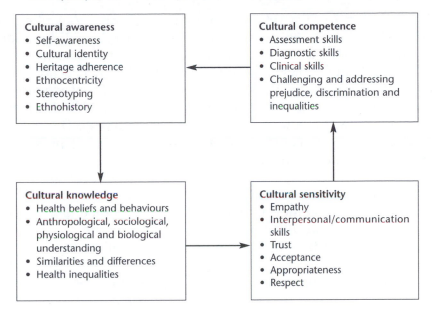

Figure 5.1 Model for developing cultural competence

The fourth stage (cultural competence) requires a practitioner to blend their awareness, knowledge and sensitivity. This will enable them to assess the needs of children and families and provide appropriate services. This stage will help them to challenge their preconceived notions and prejudices, and try to redefine their perceptions.

This model can be adapted by early childhood practitioners.

The different components of the four stages is an ongoing process requiring practitioners to revisit these stages whenever they encounter children from GRT families so that they do not plan and deliver services based on their prejudices.

Legislation

Children's rights to protection, care, opportunities for development, educational experiences and cultural identity are expressed both in the United Nations Convention on the Rights of the Child (UN, 1989) and in domestic legislation. Children and their families from GRT communities have the same rights in this country as all other children, as recommended by articles 28 and 29 of the United Nations Convention on the Rights of the Child.

Under section 7 of the 1996 Education Act, parents are required to ensure that children of compulsory school age receive full-time education, and failure to do so constitutes an offence under section 444. In England and Wales, according to the 1996 Act, schools are required to be open for 190 days or 380 sessions. However, children belonging to Gypsy and Traveller parents whose livelihoods involve travel are allowed to attend 200 sessions (DCSF, 2008a). This ensures children and their families are protected from being prosecuted while travelling for work reasons.

Since 1998, children from GRT families can register at more than one school. Pupil Registration Regulations, revised in 2006 (DfES), have enabled registration at more than one school if the child travels away. This prevents Gypsy, Roma or Traveller children from being deleted from the register of their 'base' school while they are attending school elsewhere. Section 7 of the 1996 Act also allows parents to provide education for their children 'either by regular attendance at school or otherwise'. 'Education otherwise' or Elective Home Education is being chosen by an increasing number of Gypsy and Traveller parents for their children.

Examples of good practice

Children

Provide a culturally diverse curriculum that includes positive representations of Traveller culture for all children. Provide positive images of GRT families to dispel myths about GRT families. Ensure Traveller culture is represented in the routine and curriculum. Provide activities for children to play and learn that are inclusive of GRT culture. Visual displays of timetables or activities will help children with limited literacy to follow the routines. Use traveller-related resources to help the GRT children to gain confidence in a familiar environment as well as raise awareness of other children.

Challenge and address any prejudices and stereotypes of GRT children and their families held by teachers and other staff. Persona Dolls can be used to raise awareness about GRT families. Discuss the circumstances in which GRT families live and the ways in which they are discriminated against by the community. Refer to the *Gypsy Roma Traveller Achievement Service – Good Practice Guide* (Hall, 2011).

Parents and communities

Sensitively explain ethnicity categories and rationale. It is important to discuss with the family whether they prefer to be called a Gypsy or a Traveller.

Parents may not feel confident enough to let their children attend the early childhood settings for fear of being bullied or harassed by their peers, practitioners, parents of other children and professionals. Develop trust by visiting regularly. Support families and children in the transition of children into the settings. Empower families by respecting and welcoming them into the community. Ensure parents and extended families are invited to attend open days and provide a wide range of opportunities to involve them in diverse activities in the settings.

Parents' poor literacy skills, their attitudes towards learning and their negative past experiences with mainstream communities may discourage their children from accessing early childhood settings. Fathers may not wish their sons to attend early childhood settings and prefer them to develop skills from a young age that will be necessary for their future.

Do not misinterpret any lack of interaction as a lack of care or interest. This may be due to their inabilities or lack of knowledge and understanding. Offer sensitive help where appropriate with completion of admission/permission forms. Parents may need support reading and completing forms or reading letters or reports if these are sent home. A follow-up phone call may be needed to answer their queries.

Practitioners

Inform all staff of a GRT child's admission and cultural differences in addition to their needs, weaknesses and strengths. Provide outreach service to children from GRT families to gain the trust of GRT families and to ensure children feel confident with the transition.

Provide training to challenge practitioners' prejudices and redefine their perceptions. Provide support with regard to how to interact with children and their families. Invite families (parents or grandparents) in influential positions to speak to children to provide positive role models. Encourage practitioners to develop a positive insight into the culture and lifestyle of Travellers' families.

Early childhood practitioners and teachers will be given help by TESS who are trained and have better knowledge and understanding about GRT children and families. Most staff in TESS are part-time and there is huge variation in their early years experience and qualifications.

 Activity

Invite pupils to bring in a shoe box and fill it with a few things personal to them to show what they like and who they are.

Ask pupils to discuss with a partner the contents of their shoe box. Their partner can then share with the class/small group what they have learnt from that person's shoe box and vice versa. It is a good

Continues

Continued

idea if the teacher also brings in a shoe box to share with the class. Discussions about the relevance of culture and ethnicity will be appropriate.

The Traveller Education Support Service (TESS)

The TESS evolved in piecemeal fashion. Local authorities developed a range of provision for children from GRT families at different times in response to the needs and circumstances of families and children in local groups. In addition, funding imposed by local education authorities (LEAs) also influenced the provision of services. This resulted in lack of consistency of provision for children from Traveller families across different LEAs in the country. This provision was made available to Gypsy, Traveller and Irish Traveller groups and later was extended to children of fairground and circus families and very recently to Roma families from Eastern Europe. After 2002, Traveller-specific grants were subsumed into larger grants provided for vulnerable children.

 Case study

A TESS teacher is visiting a caravan site to try to convince a mother with three young children aged 3, 6 and 8 years to access appropriate educational services provided by the local authority. The mother explains that she needs to ask her husband, who is not currently in town, and will think about bringing the children once her husband approves of her decision. After a week, the teacher arrives to follow up with this family, but with a play sack with some resources – books and stories and some toys appropriate for the age of the children. The mother and the children respond positively on the second visit. When the teacher was ready to return, the children's mother managed to convey a message that her family are not keen to send their child to a nursery or school.

As a manager of the Traveller Education Support Service, how will you

- Establish the reasons for not accessing the services provided in the local authority?
- Convince the family to access educational services in the local authority?
- Help the family to access the services provided by your local authority?
- What will you advise the teacher to do on her next visit?

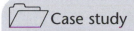 Case study

Jemboy, a looked-after child

Issues surrounding identity need to be approached with particular sensitivity. This case study illustrates how even very young children can be subject to racism because of their ethnic heritage. The case study also exemplifies what can and should be done to support children and families who experience such trauma.

Children who are in local authority care and are from Gypsy, Roma or Irish Traveller backgrounds may not be regarded as having culturally diverse backgrounds but it is important for all children to know about their cultural heritage. In this case, one of the carers shared the child's heritage and some of their experiences.

Early years practitioners can play an important role in supporting children and families in understanding identity. Many practitioners will find this a difficult area to address and most would need some additional professional development opportunities to support their understanding and give them confidence to support the child and family.

Jemboy is a 4-year-old boy of white Irish Traveller ethnicity and British nationality who was taken into local authority care at the age of 11 months. He was adopted by a white British father and a white English Gypsy mother when he was 3 years old. Initially Jemboy was allocated a placement in a community childcare service and then attended a local school.

Jemboy's adoptive parents endeavoured to promote his awareness of and pride in his identity and he had brought in old photographs of his paternal grandparents in a Bender Tent to share at circle time. Other families expressed discontent with Jemboy's presence in the reception class as a result of this.

The family was subjected to anti-Irish and anti-Irish Traveller racism, which impacted negatively on them all. The adoptive parents reported that the school did not challenge this racism; it either ignored it or denied Jemboy's Irish Traveller ethnicity to other children and parents at the school.

Jemboy's parents sought the support of the children's centre he previously attended, as they felt that, despite many attempts, their concerns were not being taken seriously by his new school. The parents were adamant that they did not want to 'cause trouble for the staff and school' but needed 'the racism to stop'.

The family had not engaged with Gypsy, Roma or Traveller communities but the children's centre provided cultural mentoring to Jemboy, via their Irish Traveller staff, to repair the damage done to his sense of worth and his ethnic identity. The children's centre supported the family in liaising with the school and local authority. They also made contact with the TESS, who had not been made aware of Jemboy's attendance at the school or the abuse to which he and his family were being subjected.

Continues

Continued

The centre liaised with the national charity Early Years Equality and they, with the TESS, provided Irish Traveller awareness-training and support to the school and reviewed the school's policies, procedures and practice with the governors, staff, parents and children. They designated a mentor to the reception-class staff. Centre staff modelled identity and rights-supporting activities and interactions in the setting for the staff, Jemboy, and the other children and parents concerned.

Early Years Equality also supported the setting by hosting parent meetings and delivering specific focus group activities with the parents who had raised objections to Jemboy's presence in the school. The school has, within its vicinity, housed and site-based Gypsy and Traveller families, who refrained from attending this school over a number of years.

The local Gypsy and Traveller community, supported by the TESS, the children's centre, Early Years Equality and the local authority Community Safety Team, held collaborative meetings between the settled community and the Gypsy and Traveller communities. These meetings allowed community tensions that had been festering for some time to be aired openly, for myths to be dispelled and negative racial stereotypes to be challenged and redressed. The school has worked hard to respect and give due, fair, inclusive and equal regard to Jemboy's ethnic identity in compliance with Race Equality Duties and EYFS requirements.

Source: Meleady, C. (2008) *Looked After Children*. Sheffield: © Early Years Equality. Used with kind permission.

Debates and controversies

Blatant prejudice against GRT communities is reported repeatedly. It has been emphasised by Phillips (2004) that negative feelings against GRT families are often publicly expressed without fear of criticism and this has been the last 'respectable' form of racism.

Appropriateness of the curriculum – does it meet the needs of this community? Communities do not want some of the curricula content that is contrary to their values and beliefs.

Hard to reach communities – what makes them 'hard to reach'? Is it GRT families or the negative attitudes of society which is a barrier for these families to access the services in the mainstream society? Do practitioners have an open and positive attitude towards GRT children and communities?

Do all Gypsy, Roma and Travellers families follow a nomadic lifestyle and live in caravans? Several GRT families are settled in permanent jobs and homes.

One of the myths that are common and controversial is that Gypsy, Roma and Traveller families are dirty. They are not. They are proud of their clean caravans and homes. They have strict rules about cleanliness with different bowls for washing hands, food and different items of clothing. Several GRT families live on illegal sites that have very few facilities for rubbish collection.

Implications for practice

Children

Provide outreach provision to familiarise children with early childhood provision.

Provide a range of resources for children from GRT families to relate to. For example the role play area can include a trailer in the home corner, transport, or pet animals.

Display positive stories of children from GRT families.

Ensure children are provided with some resources to take home and bring back.

In order to encourage children to attend an early childhood setting, encourage them to bring a comfort object.

Focus on the child's strengths rather than their weaknesses and encourage the child to develop their abilities through their strengths.

Parents

No assumptions should be made on the basis of stereotypes. Involving GRT parents and the wider community positively in the development of the school is vital to raise the profile of the setting.

Recruiting and supporting Gypsy and Traveller parents to be school governors, inviting them to work in schools as mentors and teaching assistants, and naming key staff as contacts for parents are strategies which provide positive role models for all.

Practitioner

Confront own prejudices. Reassess prejudices and stereotypes. Challenge negative stereotypes and promote good practice.

Always liaise with an experienced practitioner before a home visit.

Be aware of and respect the values, beliefs and traditions of GRT families.

Resources presented in the settings should reflect and promote a positive view of their culture and lifestyle. Develop an ethos and culture in the setting that promotes equality and respect.

Ensure practitioners and teachers attend training to raise awareness about Traveller families and communities. Provide opportunities to share good practice with colleagues outside school.

Research issues

This section refers to research published around some significant issues concerning Gypsy, Roma and Travellers families. Some of the issues that have been researched include:

- Attitudes of children, practitioners and parents towards GRT children and their families.
- Strategies used to include GRT children successfully.
- Factors influencing or impeding GRT families from accessing available services in the community.
- Barriers to inclusion and factors maximising inclusion have been investigated.
- Ways in which parents could be involved in the early childhood setting.
- Prejudices and stereotypes prevalent in the community.

D'Arcy, K. (2010) *How Can Early Years Services Improve Access and Transition into Early Years Settings and Primary Schools for Gypsy, Roma and Traveller Children?* Leeds: CWDC.

D'Arcy has investigated how early years services can improve access into early years settings and primary schools for Gypsy, Roma and Traveller children.

- What are the key findings of this research project?
- As a early childhood practitioner, reflect on the findings and relate them to your own perceptions.

Department for Children, Schools and Families (2009a) *Building Futures: Developing Trust – A Focus on Provision for Children from Gypsy, Roma and Traveller Backgrounds in the Early Years Foundation Stage.* Nottingham: DCSF.

This document raises awareness of practitioners about children from Gypsy, Roma and Traveller families on a range of different issues impacting on children and their families to access services. The document provides interesting case studies followed by opportunities to reflect and discuss.

- As a student or practitioner, what are your prejudices about children from GRT families?

- Prepare a brief presentation to your peers challenging prejudices about children from GRT families.

Ureche, H. and Franks, M. (2008) *This Is Who We Are: A Study of the Experiences of Roma, Gypsy and Traveller Children throughout England*. London: Children's Society.

This publication introduces the issues around GRT children and their families in a concise and clear manner. It will enable students to confront their own prejudices and redefine their perceptions about children.

- What are the key issues identified by children as being important?

- What are the attitudes of people towards GRT children and their families?

- Reflect on the findings and relate to your perceptions in groups.

Further reading

Brown, B. (1998) *Unlearning Discrimination in the Early Years*. Stoke-on-Trent: Trentham Books.

Derrington, C. (2010) '"They say the grass is blue": Gypsies, Travellers and cultural dissonance', in R. Rose (ed.), *Confronting Obstacles to Inclusion: International Responses to Developing Inclusive Education*. London: Routledge.

Save the Children (2006) *Working Towards Inclusive Practice: Gypsy and Traveller Cultural Awareness Training and Activities for Early Years Settings*. London: Save the Children (www.savethechildren.org.uk).

Save the Children (2007) *Early Years Outreach Practice: Supporting Early Years Practitioners Working with Gypsy, Roma and Traveller Families*. London: Save the Children (www.savethechildren.org.uk).

Useful websites

National Association of Teachers of Travellers and other Professionals, www.natt.org.uk/.

Friends, families and travellers, http://www.gypsy-traveller.org/your-family/young-people/educational-reports-and-resources/.

Gypsy Roma Traveller Leeds, http://www.grtleeds.co.uk/.

Gypsy Roma Traveller history month, http://www.grthm.co.uk/.

There are several local authorities providing useful information regarding services offered as well as resources on their websites.

Disability and inclusion

Chapter overview

The focus of this chapter is on disability and inclusion from the perspectives of children, parents and practitioners. The diverse ways of using a range of resources with some reasonable adjustments made to meet the needs of children are discussed. The ways in which children with disabilities are included and the reasons why they are excluded are explored.

The concept of disability is complex, dynamic, multidimensional and contested. Generalisations about disability have been misleading due to the wheelchair being the universal sign for disability. Whenever a discussion around disability and inclusion is initiated, the first response will either be 'Oh, there is a ramp in the school' or 'We do not have any children in a wheelchair'. A child can be disabled by their bodily impairments or by restricted access due to physical barriers. Children may have a variety of disabilities ranging from mild to severe, related to physical, mental and sensory conditions. The interpretation of disability varies in different countries. The OECD (2004) reported inconsistencies in the interpretation of incidence of sensory disability. Greece and Japan categorised less than 0.01 per cent as blind or partially sighted in contrast to 0.1 per cent in the Czech Republic. In the UK, there are 770,000 disabled children under the age of 16 years, with 1 child in 20 being disabled. (Source: Office for Disability Issues, 2012.) The Office for Disability Issues has updated Department for Work and Pensions estimates (2012) which show there are over 10 million disabled people in Great Britain, of whom 5.1 million are adults of working age, 5.0 million are over state pension age and 0.8 million are children. This relates to 10.9 per cent of the population to be disabled.

The placement of children with disabilities has undergone several changes in the past century from being hidden away and exiled in institutions. They used to be shut away from society due to stigma. It was in the later part of the twentieth century that the rights of all children to be integrated into society with dignity and respect were highlighted.

Some definitions

Disability is a wide concept and covers a diverse range of issues. Disability is also a complex concept and has different interpretations. The *World Report on Disability* (WHO and World Bank, 2011) describes disability as 'an evolving concept'. This report emphasises that disability of an individual will obstruct their full participation owing to negative attitudes of others and a restrictive environment.

In 1980 the World Health Organization (WHO, 1980) proposed a classification system for impairments, disabilities and handicaps. These three concepts have been defined as follows:

Impairments relate to abnormalities of psychological, physiological, or anatomical body structure, appearance and/or function.

Disabilities reflect the consequence of impairment in terms of functional performance or inability to undertake activities considered normal.

Handicap refers to the disadvantage experienced by an individual as a result of impairment or disabilities.

In short, impairments represent disorder at the organ level, disabilities at the level of the person and handicap is the interaction between the individual and their environment.

The Equality Act 2010 defines a disabled person as 'someone who has a physical or mental impairment that has a substantial and long-term adverse effect on his or her ability to carry out normal day-to-day activities'.

'A physical or mental impairment which has a substantial or long-term adverse effect on his or her ability to carry out normal day to day activities' is the definition in the Disability Discrimination Act 1995.

The Children Act 1989 defines disability as follows:

> A child is disabled if he is blind, deaf or dumb or suffers from a mental disorder of any kind or is substantially and permanently handicapped by illness, injury or congenital deformity or such other disability as may be prescribed. (Section 17 (11))

The Early Support Pilot Programme (ESPP) provides this guidance on the concept of disability: A child under 3 years of age shall be considered disabled if he/she: (i) is experiencing significant developmental impairment or delays, in one or more of the areas of cognitive development, sensory or physical development, communication development, social, behavioural or emotional development; or (ii) has a condition which has a high probability of resulting in developmental delay.

These definitions emphasise impairment with a long-term effect resulting in their inability to carry out day-to-day activities (DES and DoH, 2003).

What is the difference between SEN and disability?

Chapter 7 on SEN explores the differences in concept between SEN and disability. Organise the following examples of children with disabilities under the headings in Table 6.1:

Table 6.1 SEN and disabilities

SEN	SEN and disability	Disability

> Spinal cord injuries, Asthma, Allergies, Blindness, Cancer, Chronic fatigue, Diabetes, Depression, Epilepsy, Anxiety, Heart disease, Mental retardation, Reflex sympathetic dystrophy, Leukaemia, Arthritis, Multiple sclerosis, Neck pain, Joint pain, Seizures, Stroke, Hepatitis C, Loss of limbs, Muscular dystrophy, Cerebral palsy, Hearing impairments, Visual impairments, Speech impairments, Specific learning disabilities, Head injuries, Juvenile diabetes.

Some of these conditions could be a SEN or a disability or both, depending on the severity of the condition in the child. So it is important to consider the individual needs of the child before deciding on the provision and resources offered as support.

Statistics

Estimates for the number of children (0–14 years old) in the world living with disabilities range between 93 million and 150 million. In England, it is estimated to be between 288,000 and 513,000 – 3.0 to 5.4 per cent of all children under 18 (Mooney et al., 2008).

Historically children and adults with disabilities were schooled in segregated settings. In most countries, children with disabilities such as blindness were sent to schools for the blind (WHO and World Bank, 2011). The category covered by the terms 'special needs education', 'special educational needs' and 'special education' is broader than education of children with disabilities, because it includes children with other needs. Of all children attending schools 2.3 per cent are placed in segregated settings such as in a special school or a separate class in a mainstream school. Belgium and Germany segregate and send children with special needs to special schools. Cyprus, Lithuania, Malta, Norway and Portugal attempt to send the majority of their children with disabilities to mainstream schools. A review of other OECD countries shows similar trends, with a general movement in developed countries towards inclusive education. The UK education system has a number of regional differences with separate legislation for England, Wales, Northern Ireland and Scotland.

Terminology

The terminology used to represent different disabilities has been constantly changing over time and in different parts of the world. The UK Mental Deficiency Act 1913 defined and categorised disabled people as idiots, imbeciles, feeble minded and moral defectives. The derogatory terminology used to categorise disabled people explained the status accorded to disabled people. The terms relating to learning difficulties have a long history but they have changed significantly in the past few decades. A wide range of terms were used in the past such as idiot, subnormal, imbecile, mentally handicapped and mentally retarded. The term idiot was used to refer to individuals with mental retardation (of all levels) even in the twentieth century. Mentally handicapped or mentally retarded are terms still commonly used in different parts of the world. In the UK, several terms have been used to refer to people with mental retardation. For example, the term educationally subnormal was commonly used in the 1970s. The Education Act 1981 and the Warnock Report (1978) influenced another change in terminology, leading to terms like specific learning difficulties (SLD) and moderate learning difficulties (MLD). Later, these terms were replaced by learning difficulty or learning disability. Learning disability was introduced by the Department of Health in 1991, replacing the term mental handicap.

In the USA mental retardation or developmental disability are commonly used synonymously. Australia uses intellectual impairment, and other countries use mental handicap or mental retardation widely.

In the past few years, a new controversy arose regarding the terminology of 'Down's syndrome'. It has been referred to as 'Down syndrome' without the apostrophe. Many parent organisations in the USA had advocated the use of the term 'Down syndrome'. Some organisations for people with 'Down syndrome' in the USA as well as in other parts of the world have started using the term 'Down syndrome' in their publications. But in Britain, the use of 'Down's syndrome' is still popular, such as in the Down's Syndrome Association, although organisations like the Down Syndrome Educational Trust and the British Institute of Learning Disability have changed to Down syndrome in their publications and articles and in their literature, the argument being that Langden Down, the person who was responsible for identifying the characteristics, did not possess 'Down syndrome', therefore there should be no apostrophe. Although there has been some resistance to this change, there is no evidence that people with 'Down syndrome' prefer to use either 'Down syndrome' or 'Down's syndrome' to claim greater power or influence.

The changes in the terminology reflected the awareness of parents, experts and society in general. Some of the important terminological changes are:

- No single common term has been accepted world-wide to describe what is referred to as 'learning difficulties' in the UK, 'intellectual impairment' in Australia and 'mental retardation' or 'developmental disabilities' in the USA. Research communities in the rest of the world seem to use any of the above based on familiarity and preference.

- Both versions, with and without the apostrophe, are currently in use when referring to Down syndrome. This seems to be a matter of individual organisational preference.

Global perspective

It has been reported that on average 18–20 per cent of school-age children around the world have special educational needs. Over the past 20 years many countries have been working towards placing children with special needs in mainstream schools. Some countries are still experimenting with different inclusive approaches – although this threatens the livelihood of those working in special schools and the quality of life of those working in mainstream schools, especially teachers, by increasing their workload.

Policies regarding the educational provision for children with special needs vary in different countries. For example, in Canada, schools are not allowed to reject a child between 3 and 21 years of ages unless the ministry is convinced that the school is not best for the child. In Italy, if a parent wishes, the student should be educated in the chosen school. Iceland has decided to omit the term 'special education', emphasising instead single educational provision. In New South Wales, a child could be educated in a regular school. Denmark, a leader of the inclusive approach, saw a significant increase in the use of regular schools between 1981 and 1988, but since then this has declined. Australia has seen new special schools opened for children with behaviour problems and histories of violence.

The appropriateness of a mainstream or a special school is still a key topic of debate. The global perspective on integration/inclusion is not consistent. This is evident in a research study done in different countries on the practice, by Pijl and Meijer (1991), who studied the organisation of children with special needs in eight western countries and identified three types of approach. According to Pijl and Meijer (1991), some countries clearly segregate children with special needs into special schools, which they call two-track countries. These include countries such as Belgium, West Germany and the Netherlands. One-track countries, such as Italy and Sweden, emphasised regular education. A third group of countries offered a more flexible approach – a mixture of one-track and two-track approaches. This third group comprise countries like the UK, the USA and Denmark. Although, in Denmark, the inclusion movement started strongly it moved from mainstream schools to favour special schools.

A UNESCO survey reported by Bowman (1986) found that 75 per cent of the 58 countries supported integration. Although most of the countries encourage inclusion, some of the clauses added to the legislation suggest that the educational provision should be to the child's advantage. Norway and Italy have similar clauses in their law to ensure educational provision is good for the child. These are used by the local authorities or the school to turn a child with learning difficulties away because the school does not suit the child. Spain introduced an integration project in 1985, which encourages, but does not force, ordinary schools to take children with special needs, mostly children with learning difficulties. In the UK, children with moderate learning difficulties (MLD) are educated in ordinary schools subject to their parents' wishes, if it is practical, education-ally efficient for others and resources are used efficiently. All the LEAs in the country are moving towards integration, though the rate of change is slower than expected.

Italy started the integration process in the early 1970s. In 1971, a national law recognised the right of disabled children to be educated in regular schools and, in 1977, another law strengthened this. But a clause in the legislation stated that the integration has to be to the child's advantage. Sweden is progressing at a faster rate. At the end of the 1970s, most children with MLD were educated in special classes in regular schools, and a decade later they were closing down all the special schools.

The Republic of Ireland has established special classes for MLD in the past 15 years. In Switzerland and the Netherlands, educational pro-vision for children with special needs is mainly in special schools. Scandinavian approaches emphasise the rights of people with learn-ing difficulties to experience a normal life. The concept of integration is derived from the principle of normalisation.

The trend in educational provision has had its influences in many countries, for instance, on the civil rights movement in the USA and normalisation in Scandinavian countries. It is difficult to compare the educational systems in different countries because the terminol-ogy used is different. At one extreme, different terms are used to mean the same thing and, at the other, similar terms are used to mean different concepts.

The concept of inclusion varies in different countries. So the information provided from different countries may not mean the same. For example, statistics provided may be for children who are included or integrated. It is not very easy to compare the educational systems in different countries because of this difference in terminology.

Rationale for choice of settings

Parental choice of schools is influenced by their priorities for their children. If parents believe their child to have severe and multiple complex needs then they might prefer a special school, compared to other parents who have a child with mild or moderate needs and believe that their child would need stimulation from their peers and teachers to be able to reach their potential. However, parents prioritising socialisation may prefer mainstream schools. Some parents indicated, in research by Flewitt and Nind (2007), that their preference was for combined placement (special and mainstream schools) that will allow their children to access specialised services as well as to develop to their maximum potential with appropriate stimulation. Inclusive settings were preferred as they allowed children to relate to their peers. On the other hand, special schools enabled children to access specialist services without waiting lists, had highly trained staff and specialised equipment. Parents also referred to some disadvantages of both special schools and mainstream schools. Staff are unable to support children with special educational needs owing to constraints, such as limited time to prepare, poor ratio of staff to children, large class sizes, and teachers' inadequate capabilities to support or understand the child with SEN. Several parents articulated their confusion or struggle to choose an appropriate setting for their child owing to their lack of confidence in challenging the bureaucratic decisions of professionals and local authorities. In addition, they felt powerless and lacking in the skills to express their preferences for the setting in which their child might develop better. The process of choosing a school for their child with SEN or disability has been reported to be stressful even though they were supported by advice from professionals, schools, friends and family. Some parents expressed their lack of confidence and/or knowledge in weighing up the pros and cons in deciding which was the best setting for their child – a special school or their local mainstream school. Some well-informed parents seem to prefer multiple components as a combination from both special and mainstream school, allowing their child the flexibility to access specialist services as a continuum of services. This allows parents to capitalise on accessing the services from both settings. Older children have been involved in projects that have been initiated between special and mainstream schools to allow children from both types of schools to engage in activities as a small group and to raise awareness about their strengths and weaknesses, and to support each other.

Types of support provided

The children in special and mainstream schools are supported by staff such as teaching assistants, special support assistants or 'para-professionals' (USA), learning mentors and child welfare support workers, such as nursery nurses. Support staff are employed by the local authority's support service, for example, the special educational needs co-ordinator (SENCO) of the school (mainstream school), teacher from hearing impaired service, non-teaching assistant, speech therapist, nursery co-ordinator and health visitor. The titles of support staff varied from one setting to another. Lee (2002) commented:

> The titles of teaching assistants still vary, despite the government's recommendation that all support staff working with teachers should be designated as 'teaching assistants'. Some of the variation is due to the type of qualification and/or experience held by the teaching assistants and some is due to differentiation of the tasks carried out.

The titles given to people who provide support differ at international, national, regional and local levels, and the type of support provided depends on the individual person's roles and responsibilities. This support will include activities undertaken within or outside the classroom to support the learning of individuals or small groups of pupils aimed at increasing their participation and achievement.

Impact of support provided

The assumption emanating from the literature referred to earlier is that the rapid rise in the numbers of teaching assistants (TAs) has contributed to raising academic standards in mainstream schools (Farrell et al., 2010).

The roles of support staff include:

- Supporting small groups in the classroom – especially during literacy and numeracy sessions

- Working with individuals or small groups outside the classroom when appropriate

- Preparing and modifying learning materials

- Supporting individuals to keep attention on the lesson

- Monitoring behaviour of children to help keep them 'on task'.

Theoretical base

Some of the issues relate to concepts of integration and inclusion, appropriate educational provision, that is, mainstream school or special school, and models of disability, that is, medical and social. The concepts around inclusion evolved from integration. However, the confusion over the use of the terms integration and inclusion resulted in practitioners using these terms interchangeably.

Concepts around inclusion have been interpreted in diverse ways. The concepts of integration and inclusion have raised debates around the world on appropriate provision for children with SEN and disabilities.

The theoretical base referred to in Chapter 7 on SEN and inclusion is relevant to children with disabilities too.

Legislation

Articles from the United Nations Convention on the Rights of the Child (UNCRC), referred to in Chapter 7, are relevant to children with disabilities.

The Salamanca Statement from UNESCO, adopted in July 1994, declared:

- Every child has a fundamental right to education and must be given the opportunity to achieve and maintain acceptable levels of learning.

- Every child has unique characteristics, interests, abilities and learning needs.

- Education systems should be designed and educational pro- grammes implemented to take into account the wide diversity of these characteristics and needs.

- Those with special educational needs must have access to main- stream schools, which should accommodate them with a child-centred pedagogy capable of meeting those needs.

- Mainstream schools with this inclusive orientation are the most effective means of combating discriminatory attitudes, creating welcoming communities, building an inclusive society and achieving education for all. Moreover, they provide an effective education for the majority of children (without special needs) and improve the efficiency and ultimately the cost-effectiveness of the entire education system (UNESCO, 1994).

The UN Convention on the Rights of Persons with Disabilities (2008) affirms the rights of the disabled. The convention enables a shift in attitudes and approaches to people with disabilities from viewing them as 'objects' of charity, to being empowered with rights, and able to make appropriate decisions.

Problems with inclusion

Focusing on the human rights issue in the context of inclusion, several important questions have been raised: whose rights are being protected – the rights of disabled children or the rights of the non-disabled children? When disabled children are placed in the mainstream school, are their rights protected or are they exposed to being bullied by non-disabled children? The right to learning of non-disabled children is not fulfilled when attention is given to children with special needs (Farrell, 1997; Wilson, 2000).

Another problematic area seems to be the use of language used to describe inclusion. While expressing an individual's view, language also provides a strong indication of how inclusion is perceived. The use of strong language by some authors was criticised by Farrell (1997) citing one such usage: 'pupils in special schools are devalued'. He counteracted the statement by suggesting that many children in the special school are happy and they experience stimulating education compared with what they get in a mainstream school.

Further, Farrell (2000) referred to three criticisms and related problems with arguments based on human rights about inclusion:

1. All children have a right to good education and to have their individual needs met. All children's needs are not met in the mainstream schools and sometimes could only be met in a special school.

2. Whose rights are referred to, the child's, the parents' or other pupils'? For example, parents might want their child to be educated in a mainstream school but the child's assessment suggests the child's needs could be met only in a special school. Whose rights should be given preference in this situation? There have been cases of older children expressing their frustration and anger at being placed in a mainstream school according to their parents' wishes.

3. If all the inclusion activists have their way, all special schools will have to be closed. This would leave parents with no choice, hence denying them their right to choose.

Government initiatives

Every Disabled Child Matters
Every Disabled Child Matters (EDCM) is the campaign to get rights and justice for every disabled child and their families. This is a campaign run by four organisations working with disabled children and their families – Contact a Family, the Council for Disabled Children, Mencap and the Special Educational Consortium. It was established in 2006 to raise the profile of children with disabilities by lobbying government to empower disabled children through their policies as well as to access the services and support provided. The website http://www.edcm.org.uk/ updates information regularly.

Early Support
Early Support is a national programme to improve the way that services for young children with disabilities in England work with families. It provides a standard framework and a set of materials that can be used in many different circumstances, as well as a set of expectations about how services should work with families. Early Support is relevant to all agencies that provide services for families:

- hospital and clinical settings

- child development centres

- mainstream early years settings

- Sure Start children's centres

- a range of specialist support agencies, including portage services

- voluntary organisations.

See http://www.education.gov.uk/childrenandyoungpeople/sen/earlysupport/esinpractice/a0067170/making-every-family-welcome.

Aiming High for Disabled Children (AHDC)
Aiming High for Disabled Children (AHDC) was launched in 2007 and set up as a transformation programme for disabled children's services in England. This programme is jointly delivered by the Department of Education and the Department of Health. Aiming

High for Disabled Children has three priority areas: access and empowerment, responsive services and timely support.

To improve quality and capacity, the government recognises that the individual needs of disabled children and their families are best met through a personal and tailored response from both universal and specialist services. This programme hopes to make a difference by ensuring all disabled children will have opportunities to develop to their full potential. Families with disabled children are supported when necessary. Children's services endeavour to include disabled children irrespective of the complexity of their needs.

Examples of good practice

What are the different ways in which you would ensure children with different disabilities are included? What resources have been used to support children to access information or learning in the settings? How are the resources adapted to meet the diverse and unique needs of children with disabilities? Are practitioners sufficiently trained to be able to use these resources confidently?

- Specially adapted resources will differ according to the needs of the child. For example, a child with visual impairment may need information in Braille, a child with severe learning difficulties may need to use Makaton (see below) to communicate, and another child with cerebral palsy may need some of the equipment adapted, such as furniture or pencils to enhance the child's grip.

- Access to the environment – some adaptations may be made to the environment to enable the child to manoeuvre him or herself comfortably in the setting. Others might include displaying notices on enlarged notice boards or in Braille or on contrast backgrounds to highlight the words.

- Choice of appropriate toys – Persona Dolls may be used to discuss issues around the children with disabilities to raise the awareness of non-disabled children.

Some children who cannot express verbally are encouraged to use alternative forms of communication such as Makaton and PECS:

- Makaton is an approach used to help people with learning disabilities or communication difficulties and their carers to communicate with each other. People tend to use signs and symbols with their limited spoken language to enhance their communication. Makaton is used to express thoughts, choices and emotions, take part in games, sing songs, tell stories, read menus and shopping lists, and write letters and messages.

- *Something Special* is a BBC programme for pre-school children that is produced using Makaton signs and symbols. The http://www.makaton. org/ is a useful website that has lots of useful information for parents and practitioners. Makaton is used in 40 different countries and has been adapted to individual languages and cultures.

- Picture exchange communications system (PECS) is an alternative form of communication especially used by children with autism and other special needs who have a wide range of communication, cognitive and physical difficulties. It has been developed as an augmentative and/or alternative communication system that uses picture symbols. Children are rewarded with the desired response though use of PECS. For example, if a child needs to use the toilet and shows the symbol for the toilet, and is immediately taken to the toilet, the child will be able to gain confidence and develop self-esteem, rather than being frustrated as a result of being unable to express their needs, leading to display of problem behaviour. It has been reported that use of PECS encourages the child to use verbal language to communicate (Howlin, 2007). It is an inexpensive resource and can be learnt by the parent or the practitioner.

Use of technology

CALL (communication, access, literacy and learning) Scotland is a small unit within the Moray House School of Education, University of Edinburgh. CALL specialises in providing support to children in education to access the curriculum and to participate and be included alongside their classmates.

Technology is used to support people with physical, communication and sensory difficulties to communicate using digitised or synthesised voice or low technology such as pictures or symbols. CALL also adapts or provides alternative devices, such as enlarged displays or voice feedback on computer, for children with visual impairment, or specialised software to help with writing and spelling difficulties. Although CALL is based in Scotland, it provides advice and information throughout the UK to parents and practitioners on appropriate technological aids to support communication and learning. CALL's website is at http://callcentre.education.ed.ac.uk/Home/.

Professionals

A range of professionals, such as speech therapists, occupational therapists, physiotherapists, music therapists, TAs, and so on, may have to work with disabled children.

Inclusive approaches in teaching and classroom practice are based on the conclusions drawn from the research projects conducted by a European agency (Meijer, 2001). The following approaches were effective:

Co-operative teaching – teachers supported by a range of colleagues inside and outside the school.

Co-operative learning – partnership approaches by pairing peers for reading and writing enable all students to access the curriculum in addition to improving reading ability, social skills and self-esteem.

Collaborative problem-solving – teachers who have children with social, emotional and behaviour problems, can negotiate a clear set of class rules to tackle inappropriate behaviour.

Heterogeneous grouping and differentiated approaches using alternative routes for learning to teach children with diverse needs are effective.

Effective teaching is based on pupil assessment, evaluation of teaching, high expectations, direct instruction and feedback to both teachers and learners. The curriculum should meet the individual needs of children and appropriate support should be provided.

Two factors that support inclusive practice are infrastructure, policies and support systems, and shared value systems influencing the attitudes, professional values and beliefs that underpin the settings' culture and approach.

A multisensory learning environment enables students to access the curriculum through their preferred mode of learning. These methods will help all children including those with specific needs to learn with other children.

Debates and controversies

Inclusion: idealistic versus tokenistic versus realistic

Is inclusion a philosophy that is unrealistic because of the expectations of schools and children? In addition, settings that take children with special needs may claim to be inclusive but are tokenistic. Warnock argued that some children are physically included but emotionally excluded. The practice of inclusion in some mainstream schools may be tokenistic, where a child is segregated with a learning support assistant (Warnock, 2005).

Titles and terminology

There is confusion around roles and responsibilities of support staff in different settings due to inconsistent expectations. For example, support staff with similar titles may have different responsibilities or diverse roles with similar expectations.

Provision of appropriate environment

Tension between parental choice and professional recommenda-tions, and the rights of parents and children to express their choice of provision, have been considered an important issue from the perspective of inclusion.

In Britain there are different schools of thought about the best way to include children with SEN. Some theorists would argue that total inclu-sion is important, whereas others, such as Marston (1996) found that students who were taken out of classes and taught in special groups for some activities did better than those who received support in classes. Other criticisms relate to full inclusion for all children based in a main-stream school to emphasise the process of education and also the curriculum in the mainstream education. Warnock (2005) criticised how the concept of inclusion has been interpreted by different schools. She warned that 'SEN children increasingly tend to be lumped together indiscriminately' (36). She questioned some children's ability to partici-pate in mainstream schools.

Long waiting lists for children in mainstream schools

If a parent chooses a mainstream school for their child with SEN/ disability, they have to wait longer to access specialist services such as speech therapy or physiotherapy which would be easily accessible in a special school. Parents of children with SEN and/or disabilities expressed their frustration: 'system is bureaucratic, bewildering and adversarial and [...] it does not sufficiently reflect the needs of their child and their family life' (DfE, 2011: 4).

Inclusion is seen as a very positive approach by some practitioners and policy-makers, but it has been considered idealistic and imprac-tical by others. Some critics have argued that inclusion happens at the expense of the education of other children in the class. A student with disabilities in a mainstream class might need extra attention from the teacher, or might be disruptive or difficult in relation to making reasonable adjustments in the class. This could impact on other children's education. On the other hand, it can be argued that other children in the class benefit a great deal from working with students with special needs and that inclusive education helps to remove stereotypes and ignorance.

It is also argued that children with SEN are confident in segregated classrooms as this enables them to gain better self-esteem due to being in the company of children with similar difficulties. Placing disabled children in a special school may make it harder for them to integrate fully into society once they leave school. If specific teacher skills are required to deal with certain children, then it is easier (and cheaper) to train some teachers. There is a need to redefine negative attitudes from inexperienced and untrained staff.

At first glance it may seem that providing special schools and units for children with SEN is a more expensive option than integrating those children into mainstream classrooms. However, the cost of providing specialist resources and proper training for teachers in all schools is much more costly than concentrating on fewer teachers in special units. One criticism that has been made of recent practice is that children with SEN have been integrated into mainstream classrooms 'on the cheap', and that the training and special resources have not been provided to an appropriate level.

Unpublished research by Devarakonda (2005) reports the following trends based on the professional advice given to parents:

• In the majority of cases, professionals referred children with Down syndrome to mainstream schools or special schools, according to the LEA's educational policy.

• A majority of parents of children with Down syndrome chose special schools because professionals referred them to these schools.

• Some parents chose special schools due to their child's weaknesses and felt that they needed specialist or more professional attention.

• In all the cases in the study, parents complied with professional advice when special education was strongly recommended for their children.

It is interesting to note that a majority of parents conformed to professionals' advice without challenging them. This might be because:

- The advice of the professionals concurred with their choice of school.

- They preferred the 'easier' option of going along with the decisions made for them by the professionals.

- They lacked confidence in their abilities to assess the pros and cons of mainstream or special schools for their child.

 Case studies

Experiences of inclusion and exclusion from the perspective of a child with Down syndrome

Lori, a 4-year-old girl in a mainstream provision, came back from outdoor play. She took her coat off without being prompted. She had a slight problem untying the strings, but was able to unzip, take the coat off and hang it on her peg independently. Later, she walked – holding on to the handrail – up to the tissue roll to get a tissue to wipe her nose clean.

In contrast to the above, the following observation shows how the confidence of a child with Down syndrome enabled her to be not only independent but also to provide unsolicited help to a non-disabled peer, sitting next to her at the dining table, who was struggling to cut her food.

Miranda, a 4-year-old girl at the dining table is keenly watching another girl and trying to copy her – cutting food, shoving the food onto the fork and eating the food. Miranda is also chewing the food properly before swallowing and manages to eat the last bits on the plate cleanly and requests more. Later, waiting for her second helping, she looks around and realises that the girl sitting next to her is struggling to cut her food and so is unable to eat her food. So, she offers to cut food for the non-disabled peer. She cuts the food without any problem. Adults around praised her profusely for her help.

All the adults were taken by surprise by her act of support. They were pleasantly surprised because it has always been the child with Down syndrome who needs help rather than providing support to a non-disabled peer.

Reasons for exclusion

When the class activities are not suitable (this has been decided by the teacher) for Simon he is withdrawn to the quiet room or nursery to work one to one on activities which are at his level. These activities include tapes, stories, listening to music, matching exercises and activities designed to improve his motor control. He is given the opportunity to use the facilities of the nursery for play activities using role play; for example, the Wendy house, play with

Continues

Continued

cars and garage, and so on, and for activities such as sand and water play. Simon spends a considerable part of the week in a one-to-one withdrawn situation because his individual educational needs are widely different from any other child in the class. Despite being in a mainstream setting Simon remains non-integrated and works separately on a totally individual curriculum and timetable.

Attitudes to inclusion

For inclusion to be successful, it is assumed that teachers will accept students with a disability into regular classes and be responsible for meeting their needs (Westwood, 1993). Their attitude will have a significant influence on the successful implementation of inclusion. The literature reports that:

- Children with disabilities progressed better in integrated settings (Cole and Meyer, 1991; Guralnick and Groom, 1988; Madden and Slavin, 1983).

- Children with severe learning difficulties, and with Down syndrome in particular, progressed better in inclusive settings (Buckley, 2000; Casey et al., 1988; Cunningham, 1988; Harrower, 1999; Philps 1993; Ryndak et al., 1999).

- The development in children with disabilities in either integrated or segregated settings was not found to be significantly different (Buysse and Bailey, 1993; Bless and Armein, 1992; Laws et al., 1996).

- Non-disabled children in integrated settings have positive attitudes towards children with learning difficulties (Diamond et al., 1997; Maras and Brown, 2000).

Snapshots of inclusion and exclusion

- 'I am special' display – every week all the children in the room could collate their experiences of the week and decide on an experience that suggests why they are special. This could relate to birthdays or other celebrations of success – achievements of targets, maximum stars received for good behaviour, and so on.

- Story time – practitioners should ensure that all children listening to the story can be given a responsibility before he or she starts reading it. For example, if the story is about a jungle, every child can be given a responsibility for specific noises to be made or show their props of pictures of characters in the story. If the children are older, they could be encouraged to draw or colour in the pictures of the characters.

- A child with cerebral palsy struggled to stand without support and had difficulties with speech. So the practitioners gave him the crucial role of the star and provided a chair for the child to sit on in the Nativity play.

- To include a 4-year-old child with visual impairment and difficulties with balance and walking, the setting made several adaptations in the environment and to activities. For example, while playing hide and seek, rather than playing individually, the practitioners changed the rules of the game by encouraging them to play in pairs so that children worked in pairs to find children so that the visually impaired child could be guided by the other child who could see better. This enabled all children to enjoy the game better.

Exclusion

- A little boy having problems with walking could not participate in outdoor play with other children.

- Several children and their parents who have difficulties climbing stairs owing to physical difficulties or visual impairment have problems accessing their child's room in the nursery as it is on the fourth floor.

- A 6-year-old child with cerebral palsy has problems with using regular cutlery during lunch. This child has been often found to be rushed into completing his meal within the lunch time allotted. This often resulted in the child not completing his meal and struggling to focus and being distracted from activities after lunch because he is hungry.

Implications for practice

Children

Every effort should be made to ensure the needs of the child are met. This can be done by adapting resources, furniture, enhancing accessibility, appropriate technology, ensuring staff are trained on different disabilities, successful strategies, shared good practice, getting adequate support from additional staff, and supporting children and their families. Provide positive role models through books and stories, displays, and eminent persons with disabilities from the immediate community to provide positive role models.

Parents

Parents with disabilities may not feel confident enough to attend settings. Perhaps they lack experience of being welcomed in the settings. How does the setting ensure parents who are disabled are engaged in the activities of the settings? Does the setting have any policy to find out the needs of the parents of children, especially from the perspective of their disability? How does the practitioner ensure the setting is accessible not only physically but also in the information received and provided to parents? It is essential for children with disabilities to have role models, so active engagement of parents with disabilities may encourage children with disabilities and raise their self-esteem. This would enable the ideal of inclusion to be translated into reality.

Practitioners

The statistics show that 10.9 per cent of the population is disabled. It is not commonly considered a significant issue to provide for parents and practitioners who are disabled. One per cent of staff are disabled, and 5 per cent of settings employ at least one disabled person. Some settings have policies encouraging applications from people with a disability. They introduce policies that ensure a guaranteed interview scheme for people with disabilities. Subject to the candidate meeting the essential criteria listed in the job description, he or she will be shortlisted for interview. The application form is available in large print, audiotape and Braille.

Research issues

This section refers to research published on some significant issues to do with disability and inclusion. Some of the issues that has been investigated include:

- Views of children about disability.
- Parents' and practitioners' attitudes to inclusion.
- Perceptions of disabled children on their experiences in mainstream and special schools.
- Support staff involved – how do they support children, and their effectiveness?
- How does a setting support children with disabilities?
- How does a setting include parents and practitioners with disabilities?

Wilson, J. (2000) 'Doing justice to inclusion', *European Journal of Special Needs Education*, 15(3): 297–304.

In this article, Wilson articulates his frustration at the diverse definitions and interpretations of inclusion. This article presents and analyses a range of significant issues around the definition and will raise awareness on inclusion.

- In small groups, discuss the frustrations and confusion expressed by Wilson.
- Are all these valid and do you agree or disagree? Support your views with appropriate literature.

Goodley, D. and Runswick-Cole, K. (2011) 'Problematising policy: conceptions of "child", "disabled" and "parents" in social policy in England', *International Journal of Inclusive Education*, 15(1): 71–85.

This article presents a critical perspective on how a disabled child is conceptualised within policy in England. The article analyses the concepts of disability, child and parent underpinning policy.

* What are the key issues raised in this article?

* How is a 'disabled' child conceptualised by the authors?

* 'Policy for disabled children in England is experiencing a revolution' (Goodley and Runswick-Cole, 2011: 83) – critically discuss this statement by referring to the article and to the policy in the contemporary context.

Further reading

Frederickson, N. and Cline, T. (2009) *Special Educational Needs, Inclusion and Diversity*. Buckingham: Open University Press.
Hodkinson, A. and Vickerman, P. (2009) *Key Issues in Special Educational Needs and Inclusion*. London: Sage.
Norwich, B., Warnock, M. and Terzi, L. (eds) (2010) *Special Educational Needs: A New Look*. London: Continuum.

Useful websites

Early Support, http://www.education.gov.uk/childrenandyoungpeople/sen/earlysupport.
Alliance for inclusive education, http://www.allfie.org.uk/.
National Children's Bureau, http://www.ncb.org.uk/.
Mencap, http://www.mencap.org.uk/.
Parentpartnership, http://www.parentpartnership.org.uk/.
Royal National Institute for the Blind, http://www.rnib.org.uk/.
National autistic society, http://www.autism.org.uk/.

7

SEN and inclusion

Chapter overview

This chapter explores issues around inclusion from the perspective of special educational needs. The focus is on several key issues such as the definition of SEN, statistics and issues influencing the identification of children with SEN, choice of educational provision, parents' perspectives, and the role of teachers and/or practitioners in providing support for children with disabilities.

The concept of SEN is contested and has been evolving. The dynamic nature of the concept is influenced by attitudes of individuals and settings as well as policies at grass-roots level and at national and global levels. The transfer of policies from one level to another is influenced by the culture and attitudes of practitioners. The support provided depends on the individual needs of the child as well as the wishes of parents. Parents and practitioners may disagree on appropriate and adequate support provided to the child. The choice of settings, whether mainstream or special, should ensure a child's holistic development, enabling the child to develop to their full potential.

Definition

The definition of SEN has evolved from diagnosing the children to providing adequate provision for handicapped individuals.

Influenced by the medical model of disability, the 1944 Education Act established 11 categories of handicap: blind, partially sighted, deaf, partially deaf, physically handicapped, delicate, educationally subnormal, epileptic, maladjusted, speech defects and autistic. The Warnock report recommended these to be abolished as it was realised that some children do not fit into the categories suggested. Following the recommendations of the Warnock report, SEN was legally defined by the 1981 Education Act.

The definition of SEN in the Education Act 1981, is maintained in later legislation too. According to the 1981 and 1996 Education Acts and the *Special Educational Needs Code of Practice* (DfES, 2001), children have special educational needs if they have a learning difficulty which calls for special educational needs provision to be made for them.

Children have a learning difficulty if they:

1. have a significantly greater difficulty in learning than the majority of children of the same age; or

2. have a disability which prevents or hinders them from making use of educational facilities of a kind generally provided for children of the same age in schools within the area of the local education authority; or

3. are under compulsory school age and fall within the definition at (a) or (b) above or would so do if special educational provision was not made for them.

Special educational needs provision means:

1. For children of 2 or over, educational provision which is additional to, or otherwise different from, the educational provision made generally for children of their age in schools maintained by the LEA, other than the special schools in the area.

2. For children under 2, educational provision of any kind.

Some issues to consider when a child is diagnosed with SEN:

• Children must not be considered as having a learning difficulty solely because the language spoken in their home is different from the language in which they will be taught.

• Children exist on a broad continuum of needs and learning styles but do not fit into neat categories of different types of children – those with and those without SEN. The fuzziness around the concept of 'SEN' is resulting in wrong labelling, causing conflict between parents and professionals, and further frustration and despair for all those involved.

Disability and SEN

Children who have a disability may have SEN too. However, not all children with a disability have SEN. A child with a disability will have SEN only if they have problems in accessing education and they will need special adjustments made to resources or materials used compared with a majority of children in the class. For example, a child with physical disabilities is labelled as disabled but may not have SEN, but may need some adjustments to be made for the child to move around and be able to access resources independently. However, another child with visual impairment is categorised as disabled and will have difficulty accessing learning owing to their condition. It has been noted that these two terms have been used interchangeably with some overlap. However, they are also distinctly different.

 Activity

Produce two lists each with examples of special educational needs and disabilities. Check for any overlap between both the lists. How many children with disabilities might have SEN and how many children with SEN can be labelled as disabled?

Terminology

Some derogatory words used to be used to refer to children diagnosed with handicaps. They were labelled as 'feeble-minded' and 'morons', referring to individuals with a mild disability; children with more severe disabilities were labelled as 'imbeciles', children with Down syndrome as 'mongoloid imbeciles', and 'idiots' were children with the most severe disabilities. Before the middle of the nineteenth century the terms 'mentally defective' and 'idiots' were used. Terms such as 'feeble-minded' and 'mental defectives' were also commonly used in legislation (for example, the Mental Deficiency Act 1913). Following the 1944 Education Act, the segregation of children with different needs was considered to be the norm for a few decades. Since the 1944 Education Act, children with special educational needs were categorised based on their disabilities and were considered to be 'ineducable' and some of them were labelled to be 'maladjusted' or 'educationally subnormal' and given 'special educational treatment' in special schools. A lot of children were thus labelled as ineducable due to their severe and complex needs.

Additional educational needs is an umbrella term used to refer to a range of needs of children, including special educational needs as well as those of children whose circumstances or background are different to other children in the setting. Additional support needs is referred to in Scotland in the Education (Additional Support and Learning) Act 2004.

 Activity

Track the evolution of terms and concepts around special educational needs of children, and principles influencing the provision from a historical perspective. From the perspective of your local council or an early childhood setting (where you are working or doing your placement), explore the use of the terms SEN and disability, and present this as a time line. Discuss the rationale behind the identification of new words and reasons for banning terms that were deemed to be offensive.

Types of SEN

The SEN Code of Practice has arranged SEN in the following categories:

A. Cognition and Learning Needs

- Specific Learning Difficulty (SpLD)
- Moderate Learning Difficulty (MLD)
- Severe Learning Difficulty (SLD)
- Profound and Multiple Learning Difficulty (PMLD)

B. Behaviour, Emotional and Social Development Needs

- Behaviour, Emotional and Social Difficulty (BESD)

C. Communication and Interaction Needs

- Speech, Language and Communication Needs (SLCN)
- Autistic Spectrum Disorder (ASD)

D. Sensory and/or Physical Needs

- Visual Impairment (VI)
- Hearing Impairment (HI)
- Multi-Sensory Impairment (MSI)
- Physical Disability (PD)

Statistics – the prevalence of SEN

The Department for Education (2011c) reported that, on average, 18 to 20 per cent of school-age children around the world would have special educational needs. One in five of England's classroom population is described as having special educational needs. The most common categories of SEN are 'moderate learning difficulty' (24.2 per cent), behaviour, emotional and social difficulties (22.7 per cent) and speech, language and communications needs (16.3 per cent). A much smaller proportion of pupils have physical disabilities (3.8 per cent), visual or hearing impairments (3.4 per cent) and autism spectrum disorders (8.1 per cent). Boys are more likely to have SEN than girls. For example, in state funded primary schools, among the pupils with SEN without statements 22.8 per cent are boys and 12.9 per cent are girls. For those pupils with statements of SEN, the incidence in boys is 2.0 per cent compared to girls at 0.8 per cent (DFE, 2011d).

Table 7.1 Percentages of primary type of need among pupils at School Action Plus and with statements aged 4 to 10 years in 2011

Behaviour, emotional and social difficulties	28.6
Moderate learning difficulty	24.2
Specific learning difficulty	13.7
Autistic spectrum disorder	8.8
Speech, language and communications needs	7.8
Other difficulty/disability	5.1
Severe learning difficulty	3.6
Physical disability	3.3
Hearing impairment	2.3
Visual impairment	1.2
Profound and multiple learning difficulty	0.9
Multi-sensory impairment	0.1

Source: Department for Education (2011)

Interpretation of special educational needs and special needs is diverse in different early childhood settings. This can range from a child with a specific medical condition such as asthma to a child who is distressed emotionally because one of their parents is away in prison or in Afghanistan fighting in the war. Several reports point to the number of children being identified with SEN but without statements being high. The proportion of children with SEN but without statements has nearly doubled, from 10 per cent of all pupils in 1995 to 18.2 per cent, or 1.5 million children, in 2010.

Issues around identification of children with SEN

It is important to identify problems and assess and provide according to a child's needs. The identification of children's needs at an early age will enable professionals and parents to provide appropriate support to children for optimum all-round development. *The Special Educational Needs Code of Practice* (DfES, 2001) recommends continuum of provision that is referred to as a graduated approach that supports children with learning difficulties. The needs of pupils with special educational needs are met in three distinct stages. The school-based provision is described in the code as School Action, School Action Plus or with statements of special educational needs. If the provision is based in an early childhood setting, it is referred to as Early Years Action and Early Years Action Plus.

> *School or early years action* – the child is provided extra or different help in addition to that provided as part of the school's usual curriculum.
>
> *School Action Plus or early years action plus* – the child receives help from the class teacher and SENCO as well as advice or support from professionals, such as the specialist teacher, an educational psychologist, a speech and language therapist or other health professionals.
>
> *Statement* – a pupil has a statement of special educational needs after being assessed formally by professionals. A document setting out the child's needs and the extra help they should receive is in place. A statement is a legal document.

The coalition government has published an analysis of special educational needs that has reviewed the provision for children with SEN (DFE, 2011b) and proposes to:

- Include parents in the assessment process and introduce a legal right, by 2014, to give them control of funding for the support their child needs.

- Replace statements with a single assessment process and a combined education, health and care plan so that health and social services are included in the package of support, along with education.

- Ensure assessment and plans run from birth to 25 years old.

- Replace the existing complicated School Action and School Action Plus system with a new, simpler school-based category to help teachers focus on raising attainment.

- Overhaul teacher training and professional development to help pupils with special educational needs and to raise their attainment.

- Inject greater independence from local authorities in assessments by looking at how voluntary groups might co-ordinate the package of support.

- Give parents a greater choice of school and give parents and community groups the power to set up special free schools.

Contexts of inclusion and exclusion

Historically, children with disabilities were excluded from mainstream education. In spite of the efforts of some parents and practitioners, children have been excluded from mainstream provision for several reasons, such as negative attitudes due to stereotypes, lack of training, lack of appropriate resources and failure to make reasonable adjustments in the settings.

Teachers' perceptions of educational provision

The teachers' attitudes will have a significant influence on the successful implementation of inclusion. An important contribution in this area was made by Bowman (1986) in a study exploring teachers' attitudes to integration across 14 countries in five UNESCO regions. The main findings of this research on teachers' attitudes included:

- Medical and physical conditions were considered to be easy to manage in the classroom.

- Fifty per cent of teachers reported that children with specific learning difficulties and speech defects could be taught in a regular classroom.

- Only one-third of the teachers felt that children with moderate learning difficulties or severe behaviour and emotional problems could be included in ordinary classrooms.

- Twenty five per cent indicated that children with sensory defects could be included in mainstream schools.

- Only 10 per cent of the teachers thought that children with severe mental handicap and multiple handicaps could be managed in the classrooms.

Some research findings indicated that teachers' attitudes changed from negative to positive as a result of their experiences with children with disabilities. This change in attitude has been reported by Giangreco et al. (1993). The findings of studies reported in the literature can be summarised as follows:

- Staff with less contact with children with disabilities showed positive attitudes (Ward et al., 1994).

- Children with physical disabilities were easy to manage in a classroom compared to children with emotional and behavioural problems (Bowman, 1986; Croll and Moses, 1999; Forlin, 1995; Hastings and Oakford, 2003; Ward and Bockner, 1994).

- Newly qualified and younger teachers show positive attitudes towards inclusion compared with experienced teachers (Balboni and Pedrabissi, 2000; Ward and Bockner, 1994).

- Teachers who are satisfied with the support available, and the education and training they have undergone, develop a positive attitude towards inclusion (Gemmel-Crosby and Hanzlik, 1994; Petly and Sadler, 1996).

- Teachers from mainstream schools perceived that inclusion resulted in a positive impact on the children without disabilities as well as themselves (Balboni and Pedrabissi, 2000; Giangreco et al., 1993; Zalizan, 2000).

Theoretical base

There are two commonly used models of disability, the medical model and the social model. These models are used in almost all areas of service provision for children with SEN. The provision of services for children with SEN is influenced by policy-makers and practitioners directly or indirectly. These models explain the ways in which the disabled are treated in society and have undergone a significant change with time. In the past, disability was a problem that was within the individual and had to be fixed or cured by therapy or special treatment. The focus was on the impairment of the child. This is referred to as a medical model. This conceptualisation of a medical model of disability has led to segregated provision for children with disabilities. For example, according to Hall (1997), a child with a disability is given special labels such as mentally handicapped, moderate, severe, profound, and backward, and sent to special places such as special school, therapy room and toy library, which are funded by charities to provide services for the disabled children. The disabled child is adapted according to the requirements of the society. Further, Hall (1997) described the social model of disability from the point of view of a segregated child. He believes that the child is made disabled in a segregated setting due to the regression and oppression of society. He suggested that the solution for this would be to restructure the physical environment and change societal attitudes towards disabled children. Hall's view of the medical model of disability leads to children being segregated, discriminated against and devalued by society. For example, they get excluded from general services, have separate transport to and from school, and sometimes they are given offensive labels and are seen as objects of pity or ridicule.

Models of partnerships

The provision of services depended on the balance of power between the practitioners or professionals and the parents of children with SEN. Cunningham and Davis (1985) suggested three models that described the characteristics of partnership between parents and professionals:

An expert model – professionals are perceived to be knowledgeable about all children with special educational needs and parents are expected to follow the advice provided by the professionals. In the past, families did not have any role in the decisions made nor did they question the professionals' expertise owing to their restricted knowledge and understanding of their child's needs.

A transparent model – professionals usually are responsible for making decisions for all children with special needs. Parents are provided with appropriate information allowing them to be active in the decision-making process, are considered to be a valuable resource and are trained to follow up activities at home.

A consumer model – parents of children with SEN are the key decision-makers. Parents are empowered and involved in making decisions for their child, as they are presented with all the options available for children and their families.

Warnock and inclusion

Baroness Warnock was responsible for coining the term integration that extended the concept of integration which enabled children with SEN and disabilities to be included in mainstream schools. The Warnock report (1978) indicated that 20 per cent of children experience a form of learning difficulty in their school careers and so the needs of these children have to be assessed and identified. The Warnock report has been responsible for promoting the concept of inclusion in the UK and around the world. Almost 30 years later, in 2005, Baroness Warnock published *Special Educational Needs: A New Look*, which claimed inclusion was 'a disastrous legacy' (Warnock, 2005: 20) as children with SEN were often found to be 'physically included and emotionally excluded'.

This report was contested by several inclusion supporters and resulted in widespread awareness of the concept of inclusion which emphasised meeting the needs of children with SEN in mainstream schools. Hornby (2011) highlighted the confusion, considering the comments of Warnock and Norwich (2010) that were published in a second edition of *Special Educational Needs: A New Outlook*. The confusion was about definitions, rights, labelling, peers, aetiology, intervention models, goals, curricula, reality, finance, means and ends, and research evidence. In his review essay, Hornby (2011) also refers to other key books from the UK and other parts of the world that have criticised the accelerated shift towards inclusion of children with SEN.

There has been clear-cut evidence from several research projects reported in different parts of the world that refers to confusion on the definition of inclusion, while Hodkinson and Devarakonda, (2009, 2011) referred to inclusion being used interchangeably with integration in some parts of the world. Teachers in several countries are frustrated and perplexed at the expectation for all children to be included in a mainstream school irrespective of the severity of a child's special educational needs and the impact it will have on the child as well as other children in the class.

Misinterpretation of the concept of inclusion resulted in physical placement of children in the school who were perhaps excluded from the mainstream curriculum, peers and experiences, thereby supporting Warnock's comment 'physically included and emotionally excluded'. This may be due to limited access to resources, teaching or learning support assistants being 'Velcroed' to the children they support, or inclusion perceived and implemented in a tokenistic way, or due to implicit negative attitudes towards or prejudices against children with SEN and their abilities.

Legislation

Some of the legislation relevant to children with SEN from national and global contexts is presented. The United Nations Convention for Children's Rights (UNCRC) and evolution of legislation from a historical to contemporary perspective at national level is illustrated.

UNCRC Articles 12 and 13

Children, who are capable of forming views, have a right to receive and make known information, to express an opinion, and to have that opinion taken into account in any matters affecting them. The views of the child should be given due weight according to the age, maturity and capability of the child. This relates to all children and includes children with disabilities.

Article 23 specifically refers to children with disabilities and states that parties recognise that a mentally or physically disabled child should enjoy a full and decent life, in conditions which ensure dignity, promote self-reliance and facilitate the child's active participation in the community.

Education Act 1944

In 1944, significant reforms to the education system were related to provision of free education for all including children with special needs. However, the Act, influenced by the medical model of disability, established 11 categories of 'handicap'. This Act stated that children with special needs 'suffered from a disability of mind or body', and indicated special schools were the appropriate schools. Under the 1944 Education Act, children with special educational needs were categorised by their disabilities, as defined in medical terms. Many children were labelled as 'ineducable' and others categorised as 'maladjusted' or 'educationally sub-normal' and given 'special educational treatment' in special schools.

Education Act 1981

The 1981 Education Act, which followed the publication of the 1978 Warnock report, recommended:

• Children were no longer to be labelled according to their disability or condition – the focus was on the child's needs.

- Local education authorities were to have a statutory responsibility to meet children's learning needs by special provision.

- Wherever possible, children with special educational needs should be educated within mainstream provision.

- The process of 'statementing' was introduced, whereby children would be assessed by a multidisciplinary team and a statement outlining the child's needs would be drawn up. The statement would include details of how the LEA was to meet the child's needs and was to be legally binding.

- Parental views and wishes had to be taken into account when deciding on provision for a child. Parents were given a right to appeal.

Education Act 1996

Under this Act, a local education authority must arrange for the parent of any child in their area with special educational needs to be provided with advice and information about matters relating to those needs. The LEAs must take whatever steps they consider appropriate to make parent partnership services known to parents, head teachers, schools and others they consider appropriate.

Section 332A, Education Act 1996, Advice and information for parents

(1) A local education authority must arrange for the parent of any child in their area with special educational needs to be provided with advice and information about matters relating to those needs.

If a disabled person is at a 'substantial disadvantage', responsible bodies are required to take reasonable steps to prevent that disadvantage. This might include:

- changes to policies and practices
- changes to course requirements or work placements
- changes to the physical features of a building
- the provision of interpreters or other support workers
- the delivery of courses in alternative ways
- the provision of material in other formats.

Special Educational Needs and Disability Act (SENDA) 2001

This Act (DfEE, 2001) introduced new statutory duties on LEAs, schools and early childhood settings relating to assessments, statements and reviews. This legislation highlights the rights of children with disabilities and special educational needs to be educated in mainstream schools. In addition, all children with SEN are educated with other children in mainstream schools and have opportunities to access the National Curriculum. It is an extension of the Disability Discrimination Act that makes it unlawful to discriminate against children in accessing education. Section 316 of SENDA 2001 recommends that all children with special educational needs must be educated in a mainstream school unless that is incompatible with (a) the wishes of his parent, or (b) the provision of efficient education for other children.

SEN Code of Practice

The SEN Code of Practice (DfES, 2001) was introduced in January 2002 and provides guidance to LEAs, early years settings and schools. It is a guide for educators and local education authorities when providing help to children with special educational needs.

- Educators should identify children's needs and take action to meet these needs as early as possible.

- Settings should deal with children's needs in stages – matching the level of help to the needs of the child.

- Parental views should be considered.

- Settings have to produce an SEN policy involving the whole team.

- Settings must appoint a special educational needs co-ordinator (SENCO) who is responsible for the operation of the SEN policy.

The graduated approach, as described in the code, should be implemented within the setting. Once practitioners have identified a child's special educational needs, the early childhood setting should get involved through Early Years Action. If the child does not progress, the SENCO may need to seek advice and support from external agencies. This external form of intervention is referred to as Early Years Action Plus.

Statements are rare for children under the age of 2. If an LEA believes that a child in their area who is under the age of 2 may have special educational needs for which the LEA should determine the special educational provision, the LEA may make an assessment of their educational needs only at the request of the parent. Following such an assessment, the LEA may make and maintain a statement of the child's special educational needs in such manner as they consider appropriate. See Section 331, Education Act 1996.

For very young children, access to a home-based learning pro-gramme, such as the Portage Home Teaching Programme, or the services of a peripatetic teacher may provide the most appropriate support or advice. The importance of early identification, assessment and provision for any child who may have special educational needs cannot be overemphasised. The earlier the intervention is made, the more likely it will allow the child to develop to their full potential.

Assessment should not be regarded as a single event but rather as a continuing process (DfEE, 2001). The identification and assessment of the special educational needs of children whose first language is not English, needs to consider the child within the context of their home, culture and community. Lack of competence in English must not be equated with learning difficulties, as emphasised in the code. At the same time, when children who have English as an additional language make slow progress, it should not be assumed that their language status is the only reason; they may have learning difficul-ties (ibid.: 46).

Local education authorities must identify and make a statutory assessment of those children for whom they are responsible who have special educational needs and who probably need a statement. See Sections 321 and 323, Education Act 1996.

The special educational needs of the great majority of children should be met effectively within mainstream settings through Early Years Action and Early Years Action Plus or School Action and School Action Plus, without the local education authority needing to make a statutory assessment.

Statutory assessment involves the LEA collaborating with parents, the child's school and, if necessary with other agencies and/or pro-fessionals as necessary. The adults involved in this process should also seek to ascertain the views of the children and young people before and during the assessment process.

Equality Act 2010

All legislation concerning discrimination against children with SEN are consolidated in this Act. All early childhood settings are expected to adhere to the Equality Act 2010 by not discriminating against all the protected characteristics, including disabled children. From a child's perspective, this legislation causes schools to take appropriate action to meet the specific needs of children. A child who has been identified as having special educational needs is not necessarily disabled for the purposes of the Act.

From a practitioner's perspective, it is unlawful for an employer to ask health-related questions and so early childhood settings are expected to review their current policies and procedures around employment to comply with the new legislation. This Act refers to discrimination in four ways: direct discrimination, indirect discrimination, discrimination due to disability, and failure to make reasonable adjustments, extending to auxiliary aids and services. An early childhood setting must not discriminate in its admission arrangements, in the provision of education, in exclusions or in a situation that will be detrimental to the child.

 Activity

Draw a time line of the legislation influencing education of children with SEN in the UK. Compare and contrast the legislation in England, Wales, Scotland and Northern Ireland. Discuss the influences and impact of the legislation on provision and practice.

Examples of good practice

Displays of positive practice – all the children's work must be respected and displayed to celebrate their strengths. Posters of eminent and successful disabled people can be used to show children that disability is not a barrier to achieving success.

Acknowledge the strengths of people with disabilities – children, parents or practitioners. The strengths of the person must be highlighted, not their weakness. Provide opportunities to access resources and services and overcome the barriers.

Information should be presented in language accessible by all children including those with SEN. Information presented to parents of those with SEN, especially with visual impairment or learning difficulties, should be shared in an accessible format.

Use acceptable language – child with Down syndrome, child with disabilities rather than disabled child – focusing on the child rather than the disabilities. Display positive images of disability. Use words to describe people (children and adults) that evoke dignity and respect.

How do you ensure children can access the resources in the early years setting? How do you ensure all children are listened to in an early childhood setting? Use appropriate resources to meet the needs of children.

Use Persona Dolls to raise the awareness of all children about a wide range children with SEN, emphasising their strengths and weaknesses, building on the positive aspects and ensuring children's weaknesses are overcome through a wide range of resources meeting their needs. Every attempt must be made to focus on the child's ability rather than their weaknesses. This can be discussed in the form of a story or even initiating discussion with all the children in the group and soliciting their opinions and suggestions on how to help.

Books and stories that portray positive images of children should be read out to children to present a balanced perspective of children with SEN. The stories must present problems and solutions to how the needs of children are different and how these needs can be met. The practitioner must present opportunities for other children to extend their knowledge and understanding.

Share success stories of children with SEN in as many different ways as possible.

Debates and controversies

The concept of SEN existing as a single category has been considered to be a serious flaw. The classification of all special needs under the umbrella of SEN may cause problems in provision of appropriate services. The services provided for the children, who are on a broad continuum of needs, may not be adequate and relevant in meeting the unique needs of the children. This is leading to confusion and frustration and conflict between the settings and the parents of the children.

Too many children are misdiagnosed as SEN. It has been reported in the media as well as in several reports such as from OFSTED that children have been wrongly diagnosed as having SEN. OFSTED (2010) refers to how SEN is widely used. About 1.7 million schoolchildren in England were identified as having SEN ranging from physical disability to emotional problems. 'It is vitally important that both the way they are identified, and the support they receive, work in the best interests of the children involved. Higher expectations of all children, and better teaching and learning, would lead to fewer children being identified as having special educational needs' (Gaunt, 2010: 9). OFSTED inspectors found that for children with the most obvious and severe needs, access to appropriate provision, from a range of services, was relatively quick and started at an early age. However, where diagnosis was more complex, access to services was not as straightforward.

Special versus mainstream school is a key issue that has been contested by parents and practitioners. Parents relate to the issue of choice of setting, whether special school or mainstream school, based on individual needs of their children. This has often clashed with the school provision. Children and their parents face difficulties when schools are unable to meet the needs of children. The reasons may include attitudes of staff of the setting, training of teachers, and availability of funding to provide reasonable adjustment, adaptation of resources, and/or to recruit learning support assistants or professionals. The government's agenda is the driving force influencing the referrals made to either special or mainstream school.

Parental choice of schools is influenced by their priorities for their children. If parents believe their child to have severe and multiple complex needs, then they prefer a special school compared to another parent who has a child with mild or moderate needs and believe that their child would need stimulation from their peers and teachers to be able to reach their potential. On the other hand, parents prioritising socialisation may prefer mainstream schools. Some parents indicated their preference for combined placement (special and mainstream schools) that will allow their children to access specialised services as well as develop to their maximum potential with appropriate stimulation. Inclusive settings were preferred for appropriate role models, relating to local peers. On the other hand, special schools enabled children to access specialist services without waiting lists, with highly trained staff and specialised equipment.

Parents also referred to some disadvantages of both special schools and mainstream schools. The staff in mainstream schools referred to controversies around limited budget to employ support staff and buy relevant resources to meet the needs of children with SEN. They also referred to limited time constraints, restricted opportunities for appropriate training as well as sharing good practice with colleagues. Several parents articulated their confusion or struggle to choose an appropriate or right setting for their child due to their lack of confidence in challenging the bureaucratic decisions of professionals and the local authorities. In addition, they felt powerless and lacking the skill to express their preferences for the setting in which their child might develop better. The process of choosing a school for their child with SEN has been reported to be stressful even though they were supported by professionals, schools, friends and family. Some parents expressed their lack of confidence and/or knowledge in weighing up the pros and cons in deciding an appropriate setting for their child in a special school or their local mainstream school. Some well-informed parents seem to prefer multiple components as a combination from both special and mainstream school, allowing their child flexibility to access specialist services as a continuum of services. This enables parents to capitalise on accessing services from both settings. Older children have been involved in projects that have been initiated between special and mainstream schools to allow children from both types of schools to engage in activities as a small group and to raise awareness about strengths and weaknesses and to support each other.

Is inclusion idealistic or tokenistic or realistic? Is inclusion a philosophy that is believed to be unrealistic due to expectations from the school and children? In addition, those who do allow children with special needs into their setting may be tokenistic.

The identification and assessment of children at an early age can be a challenge due to the lack of resources, difficulty of access to professionals and agencies, and parents denying their child's SEN.

Inclusion and league tables – schools' outlook on admitting children with SEN, affecting competition and performance of children, may impact on the place of the school in league tables; schools hesitate to admit children who are not able to perform at a certain level so as not to bring down the quality of the school's performance.

 Case study

Examine the setting in which you are working or doing your placement. How does the setting ensure SEN needs of children are met in that setting?

Kieran, a 3-year-old child with visual impairment, attended a local nursery. The setting had adapted the nursery based on the advice of the early years consultant. For example, wind chimes (close to the door leading to the outdoor area), or extractor fan (bathroom) enabled Kieran to capitalise on using his hearing abilities to be engaged in an activity. Further, early childhood practitioners used different smells to differentiate between different rooms in the setting. A wide range of smells was used to enable Kieran to be independent and confident. The setting hoped to encourage other children not to leave any toys on the floor but did not change the room layout to prevent accidents.

Kieran gained confidence to access different parts of the early childhood setting by using his sense of smell and hearing. He related to different areas and rooms in the settings through specific sounds related to those rooms.

As a practitioner, how would you introduce these adaptations to Kieran and to other children in the group?

How would an early childhood setting practitioner setting ensure all children's needs are met in the setting? How can you as a head of a setting ensure you are proactive to meeting needs of children rather than planning to meet the needs of children when a child or parent arrives? Is it possible to meet the needs of all these children?

Some ideas strengthening good practice are:

• Ask parents for first hand information about the child.

• Observe the child.

• Emphasise strengths rather than weaknesses.

• Provide first-hand experiences to children.

• Install ramps, wide doorways, toileting facilities, lower tables, sinks.

• Create a soft play area.

• Use musical instruments to relax and soothe.

• Read stories of children in different circumstances.

• Use different forms of communication between children and adults – sign language, Makaton, Picture Exchange Communication System (PECS).

• Use Persona Dolls to raise an issue with other children.

• Provide opportunities for children to access all learning opportunities.

Implications for practice

Tension between parents and professionals – there is tension between parents and professionals on the educational provision with regards to the child with SEN. The recommendation is not always accepted by parents as the ideal choice.

Dilemmas in the choice of provision – special or mainstream provision. Parents are often faced with a dilemma on the appropriate provision for children with SEN. The dilemma is about which provision will suit the needs of children. The choice is influenced by the severity of the needs of the child and the confidence of the parents to fight for the support their child needs.

Exclusion in inclusive setting – children with SEN are given inadequate support, which leads to inappropriate behaviour, resulting in exclusion. On the other hand, parents of children without SEN are unhappy due to disproportionate support provided.

Impact of inclusive education – children and teachers have highlighted the positive influence of children with SEN. Teachers stated that working with children with SEN resulted in positive experiences that broadened their knowledge and understanding, in addition to raising awareness of children with a wide range of SEN and how to provide for these children. Inclusion of children with SEN and diverse backgrounds in mainstream schools is beneficial for other children through raised awareness of different needs, abilities and strengths.

 Research issues

This section refers to research published around some significant issues concerning disability. Some topics that have been researched around children with SEN include:

- Attitudes of parents and practitioners towards inclusion.
- Children's experiences of inclusion and its impact.
- Appropriate provision – mainstream or special schools.
- Factors influencing inclusion, barriers to inclusion.
- Understanding and interpreting inclusion from the perspectives of children, parents and practitioners.
- Links between policy and practice.
- Travel of policy from global and national level to early childhood setting.
- Factors influencing partnership between parents and practitioners in an early childhood setting.

Jones, P. (2005) 'Inclusion: lessons from the children', *British Journal of Special Education*, 32(2): 60–66.

This article provides an insight into children's perspectives around the inclusion debate. It raises awareness of students about ways in which information from children can be acquired involving parents or practitioners. The booklet used in the study could be adapted to explore what inclusion may mean for them from general and personal perspectives.

- List the key findings of this study.
- What is the feasibility of repeating this study in an early childhood setting?
- How will you adapt the booklet to obtain information from children in your setting?

Continues

Continued

De Boer, A., Pijl, S.J. and Minnaert, A. (2011) 'Regular primary schoolteachers' attitudes towards inclusive education: a review of the literature', *International Journal of Inclusive Education*, 15(3): 331–53.

This article focuses on the attitudes of teachers towards inclusive education, the factors influencing their attitudes and the effects their attitudes have on the inclusion of children with special needs. A majority of teachers held negative attitudes towards inclusive education.

- What are the key findings frequently reported though the literature?
- Do you agree with these findings?
- Do these findings reflect practice in early childhood settings in your country?

Hodkinson, A. (2010) 'Inclusive and special education in the English educational system: historical perspectives, recent developments and future challenges', *British Journal of Special Education,* 37(2): 61–7.

This article critically reflects on the development of inclusion in England and discusses the journey from segregation to integration. It emphasises the importance of listening to children, their families and professionals to achieve inclusive consciousness.

- List the key issues covered in this article.
- Draw out important quotes useful for your assessments.
- Do you agree or disagree with any of the barriers and challenges listed by the author?
- How is inclusion located from different perspectives (individual child, school, local authority and government)?
- What are the issues preventing policy from being implemented in practice?

Further reading

Booth, T. and Ainscow, M. (2002) *Index for Inclusion*. Bristol: CSIE.

Frederickson, N. and Cline, T. (2009) *Special Educational Needs, Inclusion and Diversity: A Textbook*. 2nd edn. Buckingham: Open University Press.

Tickell, C. (2011) *The Early Years: Foundations for Life, Health and Learning – An Independent Report on the Early Years Foundation Stage to Her Majesty's Government*. London: DfE.

Warnock, M. and Norwich, B. (2010) *Special Educational Needs: A New Look*. 2nd edn. L. Terzi (ed.) London: Continuum Books.

Useful websites

Centre for Studies in Inclusive Education, http://www.csie.org.uk/.
Enabling Education Network, http://www.eenet.org.uk/.
Organisation for Economic Co-operation and Development, http://www.oecd.org.
European Agency for Development in Special Needs Education, http://www.european-agency.org/.

Conclusion

Inclusion is a concept that is difficult to understand owing to a wide range of definitions and interpretations. This term provokes strong feelings that are poles apart. Some are passionate about inclusion and perceive it as a human rights issue; others see inclusion as the root of all problems especially when strong advocates blindly impose inclusion or exclusion. Dyson (2001: 25) criticises the UK educational system as 'an intention to treat all learners as essentially the same and an equal and opposite intention to treat them as different'.

Some definitions focus on children with disabilities, schools, communities, and so on. Some countries believe inclusion to be about individuals with disability, the girl child and the socially disadvantaged as they are the only groups to be excluded, for different reasons. The focus on the categories of people who need to be included may be different from one country to another.

Exposure and awareness of differences will enable children to recognise and celebrate them at a young age. This will allow children to overcome their fear of difference, and gain respect and accept the differences confidently. Inclusion relates to how children are entitled to have all their needs met whether in their home or in an early childhood setting. All early childhood practitioners should ensure they are aware of the specific as well as the changing needs of all children in their care, and meet them appropriately.

This book has attempted to explore the concept of inclusion from a wider perspective. The book covers some issues from an early childhood perspective. Some significant issues have not been included such as socio-economic disadvantage, gifted and talented, and some medical conditions which not only need medical attention but also need the community to accept and respect the child rather than discriminate based on a stereotype and exclude them. Children with HIV and Aids are often excluded by the community due to stigma.

Looked-after children, children in care, children from dysfunctional families are other categories of children who are excluded by the community.

Am I included?

There are several settings around the world that claim to be totally inclusive and include everybody related to the setting, such as children, parents and practitioners. The concept behind total or full inclusion is always subject to an individual's or an organisation's interpretation. One of the first questions that occurs is about the inclusion of children: who is mainly responsible in the exclusion process – child/ren/parents or practitioner? Is it possible to include children in all aspects of an early childhood setting? What are they included in? Are they given access to all resources? Can they participate in all the activities? Are they involved in the planning process? Are children encouraged to participate in planning their environment? Are babies and children listened to? Do children have any role in recruiting staff for the setting?

Are carers and/or guardians of children given opportunities to articulate their opinions and given the same access as parents? In this day of globalisation, migration of families is widespread due to career-based decisions, asylum seekers, and so on. Adults take the decisions to migrate, leading to children following their parents and landing in strange countries where physical appearances of people, environment, culture, language, accents, and so on are different. When children arrive in these strange countries they are expected to adapt to the new circumstances and the people, with very little arrangements made to smooth the transition.

Parents

All settings in the UK will have a parent partnership policy. Are parents included in all aspects of the settings? Do parents consider it to be necessary? Is it feasible? Why do they need to be included in the early childhood setting? Are parents given access to the setting? Are there any opportunities for the extended family to be involved in the early childhood settings? How are parents who are bilingual/multilingual enabled to access information in their mother tongue? How is information communicated to parents on a regular basis?

Practitioners

It has been generally expected that practitioners are included in all aspects of settings. Is this a myth or a fact? Are practitioners involved in review of or developing policies for the setting? The style of leadership will influence the ethos that will empower practitioners to take responsibility for the children in the settings. Are practitioners helped to be inclusive by appropriate training? Are there adequate opportunities to share good practice with colleagues in the setting and/or to share with colleagues outside the setting? Do practitioners feel included? Do practitioners treat each other with respect irrespective of their roles in the setting? Are *all* staff members invited to staff meetings, to develop and review policies? Is there wider participation in staff meetings? Are all staff members aware of and able to access relevant information? Do all staff feel the ownership of the setting and its policies?

Does the ethos of the setting encourage and promote the culture of accepting and respecting the differences in children, practitioners or parents? What is the criterion for the deciding on planning needs of training for practitioners? Who decides on the content of training days – government, council, head of the setting or a joint decision of all the practitioners? A setting cannot be inclusive just by displaying notices in different languages or multicultural resources, without using them appropriately.

This raises a big question from the perspective of inclusion in practice: is inclusion realistic or tokenistic? Is inclusion perceived as an idealism that is good as a principle but that may not work in practice?

Is inclusion a puzzle?

Corbett and Slee's (2000) interpretation of integration and inclusion, referring to the metaphor of a puzzle, is simple and explicit. Integration is about several shapes (children with diverse needs) struggling to conform and trying to fit into the system (early childhood settings/schools) which is usually one shape and size. They recommend that the system (the settings) should provide varied shapes (services) to accommodate children with different needs. The varied shapes could be interpreted as a range of services, resources, attitudes of practitioners, friendly policies and a positive environment that allows children with diverse and dynamic needs (unusual shapes) to develop to their optimum potential. The provision of appropriate services to children and their families from an early age will facilitate an environment where differences are accepted and celebrated. However, misinterpretations and exaggerated expectations, and/or unreal circumstances may create chaos and confusion, leading to frustration and negative experiences for children and their families as well as guilt of practitioners for not being able to meet their needs appropriately. Further, the complicated journey of policy from global to grass-roots level swimming across cultures of governments and wading through grounded values and beliefs of society that are embedded in the ethos of the settings, may result in misinterpretation of the policy. This may lead to inconsistency and ineffective services reaching out to the children and their families, not meeting their unique needs adequately.

Practitioners, parents and professionals, and agencies should endeavour to stand firmly together to provide support to children and each other by recognising, accepting and respecting differences in an ideal inclusive setting.

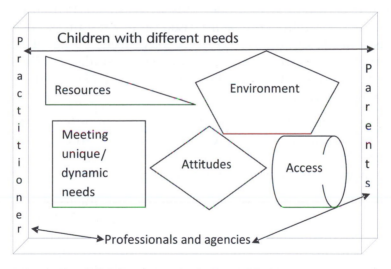

Figure C.1 Needs of children in an inclusive setting
Source: adapted version of Stubbs (2008) and inspired by the concept conceived by Corbett and Slee (2000)

Figure C.1 is a slightly adapted version of Corbett and Slee's (2000) puzzle where needs of children are encased securely in a setting with two-way or multi-way interactions between the parents, practitioners, professionals and agencies to ensure adequate provision of services.

Criticism of definitions of inclusion

A friend working in a mainstream school stated they thought they were inclusive. He referred to their admission policy and mentioned that they take children with varying disabilities of differing severity and ages, in addition to those from different backgrounds, speaking different languages. However, he highlighted the fact that they would accept only those who belonged to a specific religion. When this was pointed out to the school, they realised that it was extremely enlightening to find out things were different from what they had thought inclusion was.

The concept of inclusion has attracted criticism. Wilson (2000) has strongly criticised the definition of the concept of inclusion focusing on the conceptual and philosophical issues by pointing to a few specific issues. His criticism is of a definition given by the CSIE, quoted by Thomas et al. (1998: 15–16). Wilson has outlined the following issues:

Inclusion into what forms of life: people have to be included into or excluded from something, because everybody cannot be included into everything. Wilson questions what the contextual reference is. The desirability criteria are based on few resources, such as the basic needs of society: (1) everybody needs to be literate and employed; (2) the needs and interests of students; (3) students find some subjects interesting and useful and (4) certain activities have more value.

Inclusion of what categories of people: there are different categories of people based on age, residence, ability, gender, motivation, social background, colour, creed and language. It is important to know who can be included in what.

Parity of esteem: some of the criteria used for inclusion will result in some institutions being better off or worse off than others in terms of quality and success of clients. So, esteem depends on the involvement of clients in successful institutions. This leads to positive perception of people about one type of educational provision being preferred to others.

Equality: it does not ensure fraternity if people are treated as equal in only certain respects. People may feel denied certain rights, treated unjustly, by not being treated the same way as others or by being isolated or lonely or denied the opportunity to share. Can inclusion help to keep everybody happy?

Empirical research: it is very hard to check the benefits of inclusion. Previous research has been inconclusive and failed to establish the benefits of either segregated or inclusive settings. Some research has focused on the advantages of the inclusive setting rather than any negative aspects. Some of the research which reported successful inclusion may not be generalised due to local variables and could have been influenced by the researcher's ideology. Wilson concludes that:

> Inclusion is based primarily on ideological feeling, it may suffer the fate of most ideologies by running out of steam when social or political conditions and fashions change. We may continue to promote it, we may even – such is the fashion – be struck with it – and be obliged to make it work as well as we can; but if we are to do justice, we have also to clarify and evaluate it. (2000: 304)

Wilson expressed his apprehensions about the concept of inclusion very vividly. He has emphasised, through several examples, that inclusion is an abstract issue. His arguments seem quite logical. However, it is interesting to note that the author has not linked to the vast literature which provides examples of definitions of good practice of inclusion.

Debates and controversies

There have been several debates and controversies around the practice of inclusion from the point of view of policy-makers, practitioners, parents and children. Some of these are summarised below:

1. Is school inclusion an abuse? Inclusion has been referred to as abuse when a child is placed in a wrong setting at the recommendations of the council, choice of parents and sometimes against the choice of the children, or if the child's needs are not being met, or when an early childhood practitioner or teacher is not appropriately trained to deal with the special educational needs or complex medical conditions of a child.

2. Is physical inclusion appropriate? This is one of the most common comments and criticisms made about the way children are included by being placed in a mainstream setting but are being excluded by receiving one-to-one support from the learning support assistant. On the other hand, the practitioner or teacher may strive to provide additional support to the child with SEN or disability at the cost of other children in the classroom, which may adversely affect their learning. Warnock suggests that 'inclusion should mean being involved in a common enterprise of learning, rather than being necessarily under the same roof' (Warnock, 2005: 36).

3. Does inclusion work? This question is important as it provokes vehement responses. It sparks debates about how inclusion is interpreted. Attitudes towards inclusion and the training of practitioners, the availability of expertise and funding and appropriate resources may be some of the issues raised.

4. Is inclusion rocket science? Could it be the attitude of a practitioner that makes inclusion complicated? A parent expects an early childhood setting to meet their child's needs to enable the child to develop to their full potential. Is this impossible? The issue is complex as the strategies of inclusion that have been successful in one setting may not necessarily work as efficiently in another setting. This may be a result of the ethos of the setting influencing their culture as well as the attitude of the practitioner. It is important to recognise how to adapt successful inclusive practice to suit another setting.

5. Inclusion is an ongoing process. The process of inclusion is constant and continuous. The process of inclusion does not stop in any setting or at any stage. A child, practitioner and family should be included in all settings by all members of the community, whether it is an early childhood setting, school or neighbourhood, health service, place of worship or commercial organisation.

6. North versus south. The concept of inclusion is understood in some indigenous societies in the southern countries (developing and underdeveloped countries) as 'normal'. It is common to hear comments such as 'we are inclusive anyway', 'there is no other way around it', 'whatever we have we share', 'we cannot afford to provide specialised services but try to use local expertise as well as indigenous technology'. According to Miles (2000), rudimentary attempts to educate students with disabilities were made in India long before such attempts were made in Europe. He cites, for example, that specially adapted curricula were used 2000 years earlier, as evidenced by children's toys that were excavated in diggings in Taxila. Also, the ancient 'gurukul' system of education that existed in India for centuries was sensitive to the unique cultural, social and economic needs of the students and their families, and imparted life skills education recognising the potential within each student (Singh, 2001). However, these educational and rehabilitation practices were lost during the colonial period (Singh, 2001).

7. Is it true that marginalised groups have to be included as they have been excluded? It supports the notion that northern countries are imposing their ideas to initially exclude the indigenous communities from the mainstream services. Further attempts are

made to provide specialised services to include everyone into the big community? Has inclusion come around full circle?

8. The concept of inclusion is trendy, and is a buzzword, and the fuzziness and political correctness around the concept apprehends practitioners. Owing to the abstract and complex nature of the term inclusion, the concept is misinterpreted, misunderstood and sometimes construed as a simple concept.

Final word

Inclusion is a confusing concept due to a wide array of definitions. The concept of inclusion has different interpretations. There have been several concepts that have been considered to be politically correct, or not. From an international perspective, inclusion has been a concept that has been used in policies but in practice integration seems to be a concept more commonly referred to by practitioners.

Confront your own prejudices and stereotypes and redefine your own perceptions in line with contemporary trends and expectations.

The attitude of practitioners towards inclusion influences the success of a setting in its inclusive practice.

If a practitioner strongly believes in inclusion, then they are more likely to make an effort to include all children in the mainstream activities of the setting. If a practitioner believes that inclusion is hard to achieve, then there will be several reasons for inclusion to be unrealistic. This quote by Gandhi (1936) clearly summarises the importance of inclusion:

No culture can live, if it attempts to be exclusive. (Mohandas K. Gandhi)

References

Aboud, F.E. and Skerry, S.A. (1984) 'The development of ethnic attitudes: a critical review', *Journal of Cross-Cultural Psychology*, 15: 3–34.

Ainscow, M. (1999) *Understanding the Development of Inclusive Schools*. London: Falmer Press.

Ainscow, M. (2000) 'The next step for special education: supporting the development of inclusive practices', *British Journal of Special Education*, 27(2): 76–80.

Ainscow, M., Booth, T. and Dyson, A., with Farrell, P., Frankham, J., Gallannaugh, F., Howes, A. and Smith, R. (2006) *Improving Schools, Developing Inclusion*. London: Routledge.

Alborz, A., Pearson, D., Farrell, P. and Howes, A. (2009) 'The impact of adult support staff on pupils and mainstream schools'. Technical report. London: EPPI-Centre. Available at: http://eppi.ioe.ac.uk/cms/Default.aspx?tabid=2438.

Allan, J. (2008) *Rethinking Inclusion: The Philosophers of Difference on Practice*. Dordrecht: Springer.

Alliance for Inclusive Education (2000) *Notes for Students on Inclusive Education*. Bristol: Centre for Studies in Inclusive Education.

Ang Ling-Yin, L. (2007) 'Cultural diversity and Curriculum Guidance for the Foundation Stage in England', *European Early Childhood Education Research Journal*, 15(2): 183–95.

Baker, C. (1996) *Foundations of Bilingual Education and Bilingualism*. 2nd edn. Clevedon: Multilingual Matters.

Baker, C. (2006) *Foundations of Bilingual Education and Bilingualism*. 4th edn. Clevedon: Multilingual Matters.

Balboni, G. and Pedrabissi, L. (2000) 'Attitudes of Italian teachers and parents toward school inclusion of students with mental retardation: the role of experience', *Education and Training in Mental Retardation and Developmental Disabilities*, 35: 148–59.

Ball, J. (2010) *Enhancing Learning of Children from Diverse Language Backgrounds: Mother Tongue-Based Bilingual or Multilingual Education in the Early Years*. Paris: UNESCO.

Banks, J.A (1994) *An Introduction to Multicultural Education*. Needham Heights, MA: Allyn and Bacon.

Banks, J.A. (2004) 'Multicultural education: historical development, dimensions, and practices', in J.A. Banks and C.A. McGee Banks (eds), *Handbook of Research on Multicultural Education*. 2nd edn. San Francisco, CA: Jossey-Bass. pp. 3–29.

Barron, I. (2007) 'An exploration of young children's ethnic identities as communities of practice', *British Journal of Sociology of Education*, 28(6): 739–52.

BBC (2009) 'Call for more male nursery staff', 20 January. Available at: http://news.bbc.co.uk/1/hi/education/7838273.stm.

BBC (2010) 'UK's ethnic minority numbers to rise to 20% by 2051', 13 July 2010. Accessed at: http://www.bbc.co.uk/news/10607480.

Bem, S.L. (1993) *The Lenses of Gender*. New Haven, CT: Yale University Press.

Bless, G. and Amrein, C. (1992) 'The integration of pupils with learning difficulties: the results of research into the effects of integration', *European Journal of Special Needs Education*, 7: 11–19.

Booth, T. and Ainscow, M. (2002) *Index for Inclusion: Developing Learning and Participation in Schools*. Bristol: Centre for Studies on Inclusive Education.

Bowman, I. (1986) 'Teacher training and the integration of handicapped pupils: some findings from a fourteen nation UNESCO study', *European Journal of Special Needs Education*, 1: 29–38.

Brandth, B. and Kvande, E. (1998) 'Masculinity and child care: the reconstruction of fathering', *Sociological Review*, 46(2): 293–313.

Brooker, L. (2005) 'Learning to be a child: cultural diversity and early years ideology', in N. Yelland (ed.), *Critical Issues in Early Childhood Education*. Maidenhead: Open University Press.

Brown, B. (1998) *Unlearning Discrimination in the Early Years*. Stoke-on-Trent: Trentham Books.

Browne, N. (2004) *Gender Equity in the Early Years*. Maidenhead: Open University Press.

Bruner, J. (1983) *Child's Talk: Learning to Use Language*. New York: Norton.

Buckley, S. (2000) *The Education of Individuals with Down Syndrome: A Review of Educational Provision and Outcomes in the United Kingdom*. Portsmouth: Down Syndrome Information Network.

Buysse, V. and Bailey, D.B. (1993) 'Behavioural and developmental outcomes in young children with disabilities in integrated and segregated settings', *The Journal of Special Education*, 26: 434–61.

Cameron, C., Moss P. and Owen, C. (1999) *Men in the Nursery: Gender and Caring Work*. London: Paul Chapman.

Casey, W., Jones, G., Kugler, B. and Watkins, B. (1988) 'Integration of children with Down syndrome in the primary school: a longitudinal study of cognitive development and academic attainments', *British Journal of Educational Psychology*, 58: 279–86.

Centre for Studies on Inclusive Education (CSIE) (2011) 'What is inclusion?'. Available at: http://www.csie.org.uk/inclusion/what.shtml.

Chen, G.M. and Starosta, W.J. (1998) *Foundations of Intercultural Communication*. Boston, MA: Allyn and Bacon.

Children's Development Workforce Council (CWDC) (2009) 'Parents demand more male child care workers'. Available at: http://www.cwdcouncil.org.uk/press-releases/1591_.

Clark, K.B. and Clark, M.P. (1939) 'The development of consciousness of self and the emergence of racial identification in Negro preschool children', *Journal of Social Psychology*, 10: 591–9.

Clyne, M. (1991) *Community Languages: The Australian Experience*. Cambridge: Cambridge University Press.

Coghlan, M., Bergeron, C., White, K., Sharp, C., Morris, M. and Rutt, S. (2009) *Narrowing the Gap in Outcomes for Young Children through Effective Practices in the Early Years*. London: Centre for Excellence and Outcomes in Children and Young People's Services (C4EO). Available at: http://www.c4eo.org.uk/themes/earlyyears/ntg/files/c4eo_narrowing_the_gap_kr_l_pdf.

Cole, D.A. and Meyer, L.H. (1991) 'Social integration and severe disabilities – a longitudinal analysis of child outcomes', *The Journal of Special Education*, 25: 340–51.

Connolly, P., Smith, A. and Kelly, B. (2002) 'Too young to notice?', Community Relations Council. Available at: http://arrts.gtcni.org.uk/gtcni/bitstream/2428/5586/1/too_young_to_notice.pdf.

Corbett, J. (2001) 'Teaching approaches which support inclusive education: a connective pedagogy', *British Journal of Special Education*, 28(2): 55–9.

Corbett, J. and Slee, R. (2000) 'An international conversation on inclusive education', in F. Armstrong, D. Armstrong and L. Barton (eds), *Inclusive Education Policy, Contexts and Comparative Perspectives*. London: David Fulton. pp. 133–46.

Criswell, J. (1937) 'Racial cleavages in negro-white groups', *Sociometry*, 1(1): 87–9.

Criswell, J. (1939) *A Sociometric Study of Racial Cleavages*. Classroom Psychology Archives Series, no. 235. New York: Columbia University Press.

Croll, P. and Moses, D. (1999) *Special Needs in the Primary School*. London: Cassell.

Cummins, J. (1980) *The Construct of Language Proficiency in Bilingual Education*, in J.E. Alatis (ed.), Washington, DC: Georgetown University Roundtable on Languages and Linguistics. Georgetown University Press.

Cummins, J. (1981) *The Role of Primary Language Development in Promoting Educational Success for Language Minority Students*, in California State Department of Education (ed.). Schooling and language minority students. Theoretical Framework. Los Angeles: California State Department of Education.

Cunningham C. (1988) *Down's Syndrome – An Introduction for Parents*. 2nd edn. London: Souvenir Press.

Cunningham, C. and Davis, H. (1985) *Working with Parents: Frameworks for Collaboration*. Milton Keynes: Open University Press.

Cunningham, C., Glenn, S. and Lorenz, S. (1998) 'Trends and outcomes in educational placements for children with Down's syndrome', *European Journal of Special Needs Education*, 13: 225–57.

D'Arcy, K. (2010) *How can Early Years Services Improve Access and Transition into Early Years Settings and Primary Schools for Gypsy, Roma and Traveller Children?* Leeds: CWDC.

Danaher, P.A., Combes, P. and Kiddle, C. (2007) *Teaching Traveller Children: Maximizing Learning Outcomes*. Stoke-on-Trent: Trentham Books.

Darwin, C. (1871/1874) *The Descent of Man*. 2nd edn. London: John Murray.

Davis, K. (2005) A Girl Like Me (video) available at www.kiridavis.com.

Davis, S., Leman, P.J. and Barrett, M. (2007) 'Children's implicit and explicit ethnic group attitudes, ethnic group identification, and self-esteem', *International Journal of Behavioral Development*, 31: 514–25.

De Boer, A., Pijl, S.J. and Minnaert, A. (2011) 'Regular primary schoolteachers' attitudes towards inclusive education: a review of the literature', *International Journal of Inclusive Education*, 15(3): 331–53.

Delgado, R. and Stefancic, J. (2001) *Critical Race Theory: An Introduction*. London: NYU.

Department for Children, Schools and Families (DCSF) (2007) Supporting Bilingual Children in the EYFS. Available at: http://www.school-portal.co.uk/GroupDownload File.asp?GroupID=1084072&ResourceId=3681142.

Department for Children, Schools and Families (DCSF) (2008) *Attainment by Pupil Characteristics, in England 2007/08* (SFR 32/2008). London: DCSF. Available at: www.dcsf. gov.uk/rsgateway/DB/SFR/s000822/SFR32_2008_19112008.pdf, accessed 15 December.

Department for Children, Schools and Families (DCSF) (2008a) *The Inclusion of Gypsy, Roma and Traveller Children and Young People*. London: DCSF. Available at: http://publications. teachernet.gov.uk/eOrderingDownload/Inclusion%20of%20Gypsy%20Roma.pdf.

Department for Children, Schools and Families (DCSF) (2008b) *Early Years Foundation Stage*. Nottingham: DCSF Publications.

Department for Children, Schools and Families (DCSF) (2009a) *Building Futures: Developing Trust – A Focus on Provision for Children from Gypsy, Roma and Traveller Backgrounds in the Early Years Foundation Stage*. Nottingham: DCSF.

Department for Children, Schools and Families (DCSF) (2009b) *Moving Forward Together: Raising Gypsy, Roma and Traveller Achievement*. Nottingham: DCSF.

Department for Children, Schools and Families (DCSF) (2009c) *Building Futures: Believing in Children – A Focus on Provision for Black Children in the EYFS*. Nottingham: DCSF.

Department for Education (DFE) (2010) *Equality Act 2010*. Available at: http://www.legislation.gov.uk/ukpga/2010/15/pdfs/ukpga_20100015_en.pdf.

Department for Education (DFE) (2011) *Special Educational Needs Information Act: An Analysis*, available online at: http://www.education.gov.uk/rsgateway/DB/STR/d001032/osr20-2011.pdf.

Department For Education (DFE) (2011a) *Support and Aspiration: A New Approach to Special Educational Needs and Disability – A Consultation*. Available online at : https://www.education.gov.uk/publications/standard/publicationDetail/Page1/CM%208027.

Department for Education (DFE) (2011b) 'Schools, pupils and their characteristics', SFR 12 2011. http://www.education.gov.uk/rsgateway/DB/SFR/s001012/sfr12-2011.pdf.

Department for Education (DFE) (2011c) 'Ethnic minority achievement'. Available at: http://www.education.gov.uk/schools/pupilsupport/inclusionandlearnersupport/mea/ a0013246/ethnic-minority-achievement.

Department for Education (DFE) (2011d) *Special Educational Needs in England*. Available at: http://www.education.gov.uk/rsgateway/DB/SFR/S001007/sfr14-2011v2.pdf.

Department for Education (DFE) (2012) *Early Years Foundation Stage*. London. Available at: http://www.education.gov.uk.schools/teachingandlearning/curriculum/90068162/ear ly-years-foundation-stage-eyfs.

Department for Education and Employment (DfEE) (1996) *Education Act 1996*. London: DfEE. Available at: http://www.legislation.gov.uk/ukpga/1996/56/contents.

Department for Education and Employment (DfEE) (2001) *Special Educational Needs and Disability Act 2001*. London: DfEE.

Department for Education and Skills (DfES) (2001) *Special Educational Needs Code of Practice*. London: DFES.

Department for Education and Skills (DfES) (2003) *Aiming High: Raising the Achievement of Gypsy Traveller Pupils. A Guide to Good Practice*. London: DfES.

Department for Education and Skills (DfES) (2003a) *Every Child Matters: Change for Children*. London: HMSO.

Department for Education and Skills (DfES) (2005) *Aiming High, Partnerships between Schools and Traveller Education Support Service in Raising the Achievement of Gypsy, Roma and Traveller Pupils*. London: DfES.

Department for Education and Skills (DfES) (2008) *Aiming High: Raising the Achievement of Gypsy Traveller Pupils*. London: DfES.

Department for Education and Skills (DfES) (2008) *Keeping Pupil Registers-Guidance on applying the Education Pupil Registration Regulations*. London: HMSO.

Department for Education and Skills and Department of Health (2003) *Together from The Start – Practical Guidance for Professionals Working with Disabled Children (Birth to Third Birthday) and Their Families*. Nottingham: DfES, P6 available at: https://www.educa-tion.gov.uk/publications/eOrderingDownload/LEA-0067–2003.pdf.pdf

Department of Education and Science (DES) (1978) *Special Educational Needs: A Report of the Committee of Enquiry into the Education of Handicapped Children and Young People*. Report of the Warnock Committee. London: HMSO.

Derrington, C. (2010) '"They say the grass is blue": Gypsies, Travellers and cultural disso-nance', in R. Rose (ed.), *Confronting Obstacles to Inclusion: International Responses to Developing Inclusive Education*. London: Routledge.

Devarakonda, C. (2005) 'Educational provision for children with Down syndrome: explo-ration of parents and teachers perceptions'. Unpublished PhD thesis, University of Manchester.

Diamond, K.E., Hestenes, L.L., Carpenter, E. and Innes, F.K. (1997) 'Relationship between enrollment in an inclusive class and pre-school children's ideas about people with disabilities', *Topics in Early Childhood Special Education*, 17: 520–36.

Dyson, A. (2001) 'Special needs in the twenty-first century: where we've been and where we're going', *British Journal of Special Education*, 28(1): 24–9.

Eversley, J., Mehmedbogovic, D., Sanderson, A., Tinsley, T., von Ahn, M. and Wiggins, R.D. (2010) *Language Capital: Mapping the Languages of London's Schoolchildren*. London: Cilt, the National Centre for Languages.

Farrell, P. (1997) *Teaching Pupils with Learning Difficulties: Strategies and Solutions*. London: Falmer Press.

Farrell, P. (2000) 'The impact of research on developments in inclusive education', *The International Journal of Inclusive Education*, 4(2): 153–62.

Flewitt, R. and Nind, M. (2007) 'Parents choosing to combine special and inclusive early years settings: the best of both worlds?', *European Journal of Special Needs Education*, 22(4): 425–41.

Forlin, C. (1995) 'Educators' beliefs about inclusive practices in Western Australia', *British Journal of Special Education*, 22: 179–86.

Frederickson, N. and Cline, T. (2009) *Special Educational Needs, Inclusion and Diversity*. Buckingham: Open University Press.

Freeman, N. (2007) 'Preschoolers' perceptions of gender appropriate toys and their parents' beliefs about genderized behaviours: miscommunication, mixed messages, or hidden truths?', *Early Childhood Education Journal*, 34: 357–66.

Gandhi, M.K. (1936) Cited in Harijan, *Mind of Mahatma Gandhi*. Available at: http://www.mkgandhi.org/momgandhi/chap90.htm.

Gaunt, C. (2010) 'Special needs "misdiagnosed" in schools', *Nursery World*, 23 September.

Gemmel-Crosby, S. and Hanzlik, J.R. (1994) 'Pre-school teachers' perceptions of including children with disabilities', *Education and Training in Mental Retardation*, 29: 279–90.

Giangreco, M.F., Dennis, R., Clonninger, C., Edelman, S.W. and Schattman, R. (1993) '"I've counted Jon": Transformational experiences of teachers educating students with disabilities', *Exceptional Children*, 59: 359–72.

Gilborn, D. (2008) *Racism and Education: Coincidence and Conspiracy*. Abingdon: Routledge.

Gonzalez-Mena, J. (1998) *Foundations: Early Childhood Education in a Diverse Society*. Mountain View, CA: Mayfield Publishing.

Goodley, D. and Runswick-Cole, K. (2011) 'Problematising policy: conceptions of "child", "disabled" and "parents" in social policy in England', *International Journal of Inclusive Education*, 15(1): 71–85.

Goodman, M. (1964) *Race Awareness in Young Children*. 2nd edn. New York: Collier Books.

Gregory, E. and Ruby, M. (2011) 'The "insider/outsider" dilemma of ethnography: working with young children and their families in cross-cultural contexts', *Journal of Early Childhood Research*, 9(2): 162–74 .

Grieve, A.M. and Haining, I. (2011) 'Inclusive practice? Supporting isolated bilingual learners in a mainstream school', *International Journal of Inclusive Education*, 15(7): 763–74.

Guralnick, M.J. and Groom, J.M. (1988) 'Peer interactions in mainstreamed and specialised classrooms: a comparative analysis', *Exceptional Children*, 54: 415–25.

Hall, E.T. (1976) *Beyond Culture*. Garden City, NY: Anchor Press.

Hall, J.H. (1997) *Social Devaluation and Special Education: The Right to Full Inclusion and an Honest Statement*. London: Jessica Kingsley Publishers.

Hall. S (2011) *Gypsy Roma Traveller Achievement Service Good Practice Guide*. Leeds: City Council.

Harkness, S. and Super, C.M. (1992) 'Parental ethnotheories in action', in I. Sigel, A.V. McGillicuddy-DeLisi and J. Goodnow (eds), *Parental Belief Systems: The Psychological Consequences for Children*. 2nd edn. Hillsdale, NJ: Erlbaum.

Hastings, P.R. and Oakford, S. (2003) 'Student teachers attitudes towards the inclusion of children with special needs', *Educational Psychology*, 23: 87–93.

Hirschfeld, L. (1995) 'Do children have a theory of race?', *Cognition*, 54: 209–52.

HMI (1983) *The Education of Travellers' Children*. London: HMSO.

Hodkinson, A. (2010) 'Inclusive and special education in the English educational system: historical perspectives, recent developments and future challenges', *British Journal of Special Education*, 37(2): 61–7.

Hodkinson, A. and Devarakonda, C. (2009) 'Conceptions of inclusion and inclusive education: a critical examination of the perspectives and practices of teachers in India', *International Journal of Research in Education*, 82: 85–96.

Hodkinson, A. and Devarakonda, C. (2011) 'Conceptions of inclusion and inclusive education: a critical examination of the perspectives and practices of teachers in England', *Educational Futures. The Journal of the British Education Studies Association*, 3(1): 52–65.

Hodkinson, A. and Vickerman, P. (2009) *Key Issues in Special Educational Needs and Inclusion*. London: Sage.

Holland, P. (2000) 'Take the toys from the boys? An examination of the genesis of policy and the appropriateness of adult perspectives in the area of war, weapon and superhero play', *Citizenship, Social and Economic Education*, 4(2): 92–108.

Holland, P. (2003) *We Don't Play with Guns Here: War, Weapon and Superhero Play in the*

Early Years. Maidenhead: Open University Press.

Hornby, G. (1999) 'Inclusion or delusion: can one size fit all?', *Support for Learning*, 14(4): 152–7.

Hornby, G. (2011) 'Inclusive education for children with special educational needs: a critique', *International Journal of Disability, Development and Education*, 58(3): 321–9.

Horowitz, R.E. (1939) 'Racial aspects of self-identification in nursery school children', *Journal of Psychology*, 7: 91–9.

Jones, P. (2005) 'Inclusion: lessons from the children', *British Journal of Special Education*, 32(2), 60–66.

Jordan, E. (2001) 'Interrupted learning: the Traveller paradigm', *Support for Learning*, 16: 128–34.

Kahn, T. (2006) *Involving Fathers in Early Years Settings: Evaluating Four Models for Effective Practice Development*. London: Pre-school Learning Alliance.

Karmiloff, K. and Karmiloff-Smith, A. (2011) 'Native tongues', *Nursery World*, 111(4260): 14–16.

Kidd, R. and Hornby, G. (1993) 'Transfer from special to mainstream', *British Journal of Special Education*, 20(1): 17–19.

Klug, B. and Whitfield, P. (2003) *Widening the Circle: Culturally Relevant Pedagogy for American Indian Children*. New York: Routledge and Falmer.

Kohlberg, L. (1966) 'A cognitive-developmental analysis of children's sex-role concepts and attitudes', in E. Maccoby *The Development of Sex Differences*, pp 82–172. Stanford, CA: Stanford University Press.

Lane, J. (2006a) 'Right from the start: a commissioned study of antiracism, learning and the early years', Focus Institute on Rights and Social Transformation (FIRST). Available at: www.focus-first.co.uk.

Lane, J. (2006b) 'Some suggested information/resources that may be helpful in working for racial equality in the early years'. Available at: www.childrenwebmag.com/articles/child-care-articles/racial-equality-information-for-early-years-workers.

Lane, J. (2008) *Young Children and Racial Justice: Taking Action for Racial Equality in the Early Years – Understanding the Past, Thinking about the Present, Planning for the Future*. London: National Children's Bureau.

Lao, C. (2004) 'Parents' attitudes towards Chinese English bilingual education and Chinese language use', *Bilingual Research Journal*, 28: 99–134.

Lasker, B. (1929) *Race Attitudes in Children*. New York: Holt.

Laws, G., Taylor, M., Bennie, S. and Buckley, S. (1996) 'Classroom behaviour, language competence and the acceptance of children with Down syndrome by their mainstream peers', *Down Syndrome Research and Practice*, 4: 100–109.

Lee, B. (2002) *Teaching Assistants in Schools: The Current State of Play*. Report 34. Slough: National Foundation for Educational Research.

Lindon, J. (n.d.) 'Cultural diversity in the early years'. Available at: http://www.communityplaythings.co.uk/resources/articles/cultural-diversity.html.

Lindsay, G., Pather, S. and Strand, S. (2006) *Special Educational Needs and Ethnicity: Issues of Over-and-Under-Representation*. DfES Reseach Brief, no. RB757. Available at: http://www.dfes.gov.uk/research/data/uploadfiles/RB757.pdf.

Lloyd, G. and Stead, J. (2001) '"The boys and girls not calling me names and the teachers to believe me". Name calling and the experiences of Travellers in school', *Children & Society*, 15: 361–74.

MacNaughton, G. (2000) *Rethinking Gender in Early Childhood Education*. London: Sage.

MacNaughton, G. and Davis, K. (eds) (2009) *Race and Early Childhood Education: An International Approach to Identity, Politics, and Pedagogy*. New York: Palgrave Macmillan.

Madden, N.A. and Slevin, R.E. (1983)'Mainstreaming students with mild handicaps: academic and social outcomes', *Review of Educational Research*, 53: 519–69.

Maras, P. and Brown, R. (2000) 'Effects of different forms of school contact on children's attitudes toward disabled and non-disabled peers', *British Journal of Educational Psychology*, 337–51.

Marston, D. (1996) 'A comparison of inclusion only, pull-out only, and combined service models for students with mild disabilities', *Journal of Special Education*, 30(2): 121–32.

Mason, M. (2004) Director of Alliance for Inclusive Education. *All Our Children Belong* edited by A. Broomfield. Available at: http//www.hiproweb.org/fileadmin/cdroms/Education/AllOurChildrenbelong.pdf.

Maylor, U., Smart, S., Kuyok, K.A. and Ross, A. (2009) *Black Children's Achievement Programme Evaluation*. Research report DCSF-RR177. London: DCSF.

Meijer, C.J.W. (ed.) (2001) *Inclusive Education and Effective Classroom Practices*. Middelfart: European Agency for Development in Special Needs Education.

Meleady. C (2008) *Looked after Children*. Sheffield: Early Years Equality.

Miles, M. (2000) 'Disability in South Asia – millennium to millennium', *Asia Pacific Disability Rehabilitation Journal*, 11(1): 1–10.

Milner, D. (1983) *Children and Race*. London: Sage.

Mooney, A., Owen, C. and Statham, J. (2008) *Disabled Children: Numbers, Characteristics and Local Service Provision*. London: DCSF.

Moss, P. (2003) 'Who is the worker in services for young children?', *Children in Europe*, 5: 2–5.

Munroe, R.H., Shimmin, H.S. and Munroe, R.L. (1984) 'Gender understanding and sex role preferences in four cultures', *Developmental Psychology*, 20: 673–82.

Nutbrown, C. and Clough, P. (2006) *Inclusion in the Early Years*. London: Sage.

Oberhuemer, P. (2011) 'The early childhood education workforce in Europe between divergencies and emergencies?', *International Journal of Child Care and Education Policy*, 5(1): 55–63.

OECD (1999) *Inclusion Education at Work – Students with Disabilities in Mainstream Schools*. Paris: OECD.

OECD (2004) *Learning for Tomorrow's World: First Results from PISA 2003*. Paris: OECD.

Office for National Statistics (ONS) (2011a) 'Census questionnaire content'. Available at: http://www.ons.gov.uk/ons/guide-method/census/2011/the-2011-census/2011-census-questionnaire-content/index.html.

Office for National Statistics (ONS) (2011b) 'Statistical bulletin: annual mid-year population estimates 2010'. Available at: http://www.ons.gov.uk/ons/rel/pop-estimate/population-estimates-for-uk—england-and-wales—scotland-and-northern-ireland/mid-2010-population-estimates/index.html.

Office for Disability Issues (2012) *Disability Facts and Figures*, available at http://odi.dwp.gov.uk/disability-statistics-and-research/disability-facts-and-figures.php#gd

OFSTED (2000) Inspection Quality Division. *Evaluating Educational Inclusion*. London: Office for Standards in Education. Available at: http://www.ofsted.gov.uk/resources/evaluating-educational-inclusion-guidance-for-inspectors-and-schools.

OFSTED (2010) *Special Educational Needs and Disability Review*. London: OFSTED.

Papadopoulos, I. (2006) 'The Papadopoulos, Tilki and Taylor model of developing cultural competence', in I. Papadopoulos, *Transcultural Health and Social Care: Developing Culturally Competent Practitioners*. Oxford: Elsevier.

Peeters, M. (2007) 'Including men in early childhood education: insights from the European experience', *NZ Research in Early Childhood Education*, 10: 15–24.

Peters, M., Seeds, K., Goldstein, A. and Coleman, N. (2008) *Parental Involvement in Children's Education 2007*. Research report RR034. Nottingham: DCSF.

Petley, H. and Sadler, J. (1996) 'The integration of children with Down syndrome in mainstream schools: teacher knowledge, needs, attitudes and expectations', *Down Syndrome Research and Practice*, 4, 15–24.

Phillips, T. (2004) quoted by BBC News (2004) *CRE Examines Treatment of Gypsies* http://news.bbc.co.uk/1/hi/england/3751214.stm

Philps, C.E. (1993) 'A comparative study of the academic achievement and language development of children with Down syndrome and placed in mainstream and special schools'. Unpublished M.Phil. dissertation, University of Wolverhampton.

Pijl, J.S. and Meijer, C.J.W. (1991) 'Does integration count for much? An analysis of the practices of integration in eight countries', *European Journal of Special Needs Education*, 6: 100–111.

Pike, R. (2011) *Patterns of Pay: Results of the Annual Survey of Earnings 1997 to 2010, Economics and Labour Market Review*. London: Office for National Statistics.

Plowden Report (1967) Children and Their Primary Schools. A Report of the Central Advisory Council for Education (England), 1. London: HMSO.

Riddell, S., Tisdall, K. and Kane, J. (2006) *Literature Review of Educational Provision for Pupils with Additional Support Needs*. Edinburgh: Scottish Executive Social Research. Available at: http://www.scotland.gov.uk/Resource/Doc/152146/0040954.pdf.

Risman, B.J. and Myers, K. (1997) 'As the twig is bent: children reared in feminist households', *Qualitative Sociology*, 20(2): 229–52.

Roberts-Holmes, G.P. (2011) 'Working with men as colleagues in the early years: issues and ways forward', in L. Miller and C. Cable (eds), *Professionalisation, Leadership and Management in the Early Years*. London: Sage. pp. 119–33.

Robinson, K. and Diaz, C. (2006) *Diversity and Difference in Early Childhood Education: Issues for Theory and Practice*. Maidenhead: Open University Press.

Rogers, S. (2011) 'The ethnic population of England and Wales broken down by local authority', *Guardian*, 18 May. Available at: http://www.guardian.co.uk/news/datablog/2011/may/18/ethnic-population-england-wales.

Rosenthal, M. (2000) 'Home to early childhood service: an ecological perspective', *Childrenz Issues*, 4(1): 7–15.

Ryndak, D.L., Morrison, A.P. and Sommerstein, L. (1999) 'Literacy before and after inclusion in general education settings: a case study', *The Association for Persons with Severe Handicaps*, 24: 5–22.

Sarathchandra, K.A.D.P. (2008) 'Young children learning for sustainable development through traditional culture', in P. Samuelsson and Y. Kaga (eds), *The Contribution of Early Childhood Education to a Sustainable Society*. Paris: UNESCO.

Save the Children (2006) *Working Towards Inclusive Practice: Gypsy and Traveller Cultural Awareness Training and Activities for Early Years Settings*. London: Save the Children.

Save the Children (2007) *Early Years Outreach Practice, Supporting Early Years Practitioners Working with Gypsy, Roma and Traveller Families*. London: Save the Children.

Schneider, C. (2009) 'Equal is not enough – current issues in inclusive education in the eyes of children', *International Journal of Education*, 1(1): E1. Available at: http://www.macrothink.org/journal/index.php/ije/article/view/101/47.

Sharma, K. (2010) 'Female literacy educating India'. Available at: http://www.indiatogether.org/2010/feb/ksh-educate.htm.

Shepherd, J. (2010) 'Girls think they are cleverer than boys from age four', *Guardian*, 1 September. Available at: http://www.guardian.co.uk/education/2010/sep/01/girls-boys-schools-gender-gap/print.

Sigel, I.E., McGillicuddy-DeLisi, A.V. and Goodnow, J. (eds), *Parental Belief Systems: The Psychological Consequences for Children*. 2nd edn. Hillsdale, NJ: Erlbaum.

Singh, R. (2001) 'Need of the hour – a paradigm shift in education'. Paper presented at the North South Dialogue on Inclusive Education, Mumbai, 28 February–3 March, 2001.

Siraj-Blatchford, I. (1994) The Early Years: Laying the Foundations for Racial Equality. Stoke-on-Trent: Trentham Books.

Siraj-Blatchford, I. and Clarke, P. (2000) *Supporting Identity, Diversity and Language in the Early Years*. Buckingham: Open University Press.

Stubbs, S. (2002) *Inclusive Education: Where There Are Few Resources*. Oslo: Atlas Alliance.

Stubbs, S. (2008) *Inclusive Education: Where there are Few Resources*. 2nd edn. Oslo, Norway: Atlas Alliance. http://www.eenet.org.uk/resources/docs/IE%20few%20resources%202008.pdf.

Stuurman, S. (2000) 'François Bernier and the invention of racial classification', *History Workshop Journal*, Autumn (50): 1–21.

Sumsion, J. (2005) 'Male teachers in early childhood education: issues and case study', *Early Childhood Research Quarterly*, 20: 109–23.

Swann Report (1983) *Education for All*. London: HMSO.

Swann Report (1985) *Education for All: The Report of the Committee of Enquiry into the Education of Children from Ethnic Minority Groups*. London: HMSO.

Sylva, K., Melhuish, E., Sammons, P., Siraj-Blatchford, I. and Taggart, B. (2004) *The Effective Provision of Pre-School Education (EPPE) Project: Final Report*. London: DfES. Available at: http://www.surestart.gov.uk/publications/?Document=1160 (accessed 10 January 2008).

Sylva, K., Melhuish, E., Sammons, P., Siraj-Blatchford, I. and Taggart, B. with Hunt, S., Jelicic, H., Barreau, S., Grabbe, Y., Smees, R. and Welcomme, W. (2009) *Final Report from the Primary Phase: Pre-school, School, and Family Influences on Children's Development During Key Stage 2 (age 7–11), (Effective Pre-School and Primary Education 3–11 project (EPPE 3–11))*, London: DCSF/Institute of Education, University of London.

Targowska, A.U. (2001) 'Exploring young childrens "racial" attitudes in an Australian context – the link between research and practice'. Paper presented at AARE 2001 Conference, Melbourne, Australia.

Thomas, G., Walker, D. and Webb, J. (1998) *The Making of the Inclusive School*. London: Routledge.

Thorne, B. (1993) *Gender Play: Girls and Boys in School*. New Brunswick, NJ: Rutgers University Press.

Tickell, C. (2011) *The Early Years: Foundations for Life, Health and Learning. An Independent Report on the Early Years Foundation Stage to Her Majesty's Government*. London: DFE.

Trompenaars, F. and Hampden-Turner, C. (1998) *Riding the Waves of Culture: Understanding Cultural Diversity in Business*. 2nd edn. Chicago, IL: Irwin.

UK Border Agency Business Plan April 2011 – March 2015. Available at: http://www.ukba.homeoffice.gov.uk/sitecontent/documents/aboutus/uk-border-agency-business-plan/business-plan/ukba-business-plan?View=Binary.

UNESCO (1994) *The Salamanca Statement and Frameworks For Action on Special Needs Education*. Paris: UNESCO.

UNESCO (2000) *Inclusive Education and Education for All: A Challenge and a Vision*. Paris: UNESCO.

UNESCO (2009) *New Edition of UNESCO Atlas of the World's Languages in Danger*. Available at: http://portal.unesco.org/ci/en/ev.php-URL_ID=28377&URL_DO=DO_TOPIC&URL_SECTION=201.html.

UNESCO (2011) *Atlas of the World's Languages in Danger*. Paris: UNESCO.

UNICEF (2011a) *Disparities in Education in South Asia – A Resource Tool Kit*. Kathmandu: UNICEF.

UNICEF (2011b) *The State of the World's Children*. New York: UNICEF.

United Nations (UN) (1989) *Convention on the Rights of the Child*. New York: United Nations.

United Nations (UN) (2006) *Convention on the Rights of Persons with Disabilities*. Geneva: United Nations. Available at: http://www2.ohchr.org/english/law/disabilities-convention.htm (accessed 10 March 2011).

UN Convention on the rights of persons with disabilities – a major step forward in promoting and protecting rights. Geneva: World Health Organization, 2007.

Ureche, H. and Franks, M. (2008) *This Is Who We Are: A Study of the Experiences of Roma, Gypsy and Traveller Children Throughout England*. London: Children's Society.

Vandenbroeck, M., Roets, G. and Snoeck, A. (2009) 'Immigrant mothers crossing borders: nomadic identities and multiple belongings in early childhood education', *European Early Childhood Education Research Journal*, 17(2): 203–16.

Vygotsky, L. (1978) *Mind in Society*. Cambridge, MA: Harvard University Press.

Wallop, H. (2011) 'Population growth of last decade driven by non-white British', *Telegraph*, 18 May. Available at: http://www.telegraph.co.uk/news/politics/8521215/Population-growth-of-last-decade-driven-by-non-white-British.html.

Ward, J.C. and Bockner, S. (1994) 'A question of attitudes: integrating children with disabilities into regular classrooms', *British Journal of Special Education*, 9, 246–60.

Warnock, M. (1978) *Report of the Committee of Enquiry into the Education of Handicapped Children and Young People*. London: HMSO.

Warnock, M. (2005) *Special Educational Needs: A New Look*. London: Philosophy of Education Society of Great Britain.

Warnock, M. and Norwich, B. (2010) *Special Educational Needs: A New Look*. 2nd edn. L. Terzi (ed.). London: Continuum.

Westwood, P. (1993) *Commonsense Methods for Children with Special Needs*. London: Routledge.

Wilkin, A., Derrington, A., White, R., Martin, K., Foster, B., Kinder, K. and Rutt, S. (2010) 'Improving the outcomes for Gypsy, Roma and Traveller pupils: final report', Research report DFE-RR043. Windsor: National Foundation for Educational Research.

Wilson, J. (2000) 'Doing justice to inclusion', *European Journal of Special Needs Education*, 15(3): 297–304.

Winters, H. (1994) cited by Cantwell, A.M. (1994) 'Howard Dalton Winters: In memoriam'. Unpublished manuscript, Midwest Archaeological Conference. 9–12 November, 1994.

World Health Organization (WHO) (1980) *International Classification of Impairments, Disabilities, and Handicaps*. Geneva: World Health Organization.

World Health Organization (WHO) (2002) *Integrating Gender Perspectives into the Work of WHO*. Geneva: WHO.

Zalizan, M.J. (2000) 'Perceptions of inclusive practices: the Malaysian perspective', *Educational Review*, 52: 187–95.

Zephaniah, B. (2000) *Wicked World*. London: Puffin Books.

Zealey, C. (1995) *The Importance of Names in Coordinate Collection*. London: National Early Years Network.

Index

Added to a page number 'f' denotes a figure and 't' denotes a table.